PRAISE
REBUILDING

"*Rebuilding Beautiful* takes you on a journey of compassion and hope that helps you pick up the broken pieces in your life and put them back together. It's filled with hard-earned wisdom and life-giving inspiration that encourages you to seize the season that God has given you and find joy along the way."

—BRITTANY PRICE BROOKER, MOM, WIFE, WIDOW, COMMUNICATOR, CHAOS COORDINATOR, SPEAKER, BLOGGER, SINGER-SONGWRITER

"Kayla has been a friend of mine for a long time, and she is equal parts kind, sensitive, and absolutely ferocious. She loves God and her family passionately and has written another beautiful book. It is a kind and hopeful invitation to us to warm our hands by the embers of whatever may have felt like it burned down in our lives."

—BOB GOFF, *NEW YORK TIMES* BESTSELLING AUTHOR AND CHIEF BALLOON INFLATOR AT LOVE DOES

"*Rebuilding Beautiful* is a tender, tenacious, and at times painfully vulnerable invitation for us to dare to dream again when life has cast us on the shores of devastation. Kayla's eloquent words are seasoned and tempered by her own encounters with loss. You will find her a faithful guide during seasons of pain and loss. Each chapter is a dose of courage to help you get up, put one foot in front of the other, and walk forward in hope while honoring the painful lessons of the past."

—LISA BEVERE, *NEW YORK TIMES* BESTSELLING AUTHOR

"*Rebuilding Beautiful* is a compelling message of resilience. A road map of hope for anyone who has ever wondered how to begin again when it feels as though life has led them to a dead end. It will inspire you to embrace your pain as a pathway to a new kind of beautiful life."

—ED MYLETT, GLOBAL SPEAKER, BESTSELLING
AUTHOR, AND HOST OF *TOP-RATED PODCAST*

"What a gift *Rebuilding Beautiful* is to every heart that reads it! The love poured into every page directs the searching soul to comfort in God but also declares a battle cry of hope over the darkest seasons of loss. I love Kayla Stoecklein and the profound and practical way she shares truth. There is an anointing on her life to illuminate the faithfulness of Jesus in the midst of unimaginable loss. Kayla's transparency brings freedom and a radical perspective shift that 'the deeply painful journey of rebuilding a beautiful life is also hope-filled.'"

—DAWNCHERÉ WILKERSON, LEAD COPASTOR,
VOUS CHURCH, MIAMI, FLORIDA

REBUILDING BEAUTIFUL

WELCOME
WHAT IS,
DARE TO
DREAM AGAIN,

REBUILDING
BEAUTIFUL

AND STEP
BRAVELY
INTO WHAT
COULD BE

KAYLA STOECKLEIN

NELSON
BOOKS
An Imprint of Thomas Nelson

Published in Nashville, Tennessee, by Nelson Books, an imprint of Thomas Nelson. Nelson Books and Thomas Nelson are registered trademarks of HarperCollins Christian Publishing, Inc.

Author is represented by Whitney Gossett of Content Capital, LLC dba, Capital Literary. PO Box 160114 Austin TX 78716

Unless otherwise noted, Scripture quotations are taken from the Holy Bible, New International Version®, NIV®. Copyright © 1973, 1978, 1984, 2011 by Biblica, Inc.® Used by permission of Zondervan. All rights reserved worldwide. www.zondervan.com. The "NIV" and "New International Version" are trademarks registered in the United States Patent and Trademark Office by Biblica, Inc.®

Scripture quotations marked MSG are taken from THE MESSAGE. Copyright © 1993, 2002, 2018 by Eugene H. Peterson. Used by permission of NavPress. All rights reserved. Represented by Tyndale House Publishers, a Division of Tyndale House Ministries.

Scripture quotations marked NLT are taken from the Holy Bible, New Living Translation. Copyright © 1996, 2004, 2015 by Tyndale House Foundation. Used by permission of Tyndale House Ministries, Carol Stream, Illinois 60188. All rights reserved.

Scripture quotations marked ESV are taken from the ESV® Bible (The Holy Bible, English Standard Version®). Copyright © 2001 by Crossway, a publishing ministry of Good News Publishers. Used by permission. All rights reserved.

Scripture quotations marked THE VOICE are taken from The Voice™. Copyright © 2012 by Ecclesia Bible Society. Used by permission. All rights reserved.

Thomas Nelson titles may be purchased in bulk for educational, business, fundraising, or sales promotional use. For information, please e-mail SpecialMarkets@ThomasNelson.com.

Any internet addresses, phone numbers, or company or product information printed in this book are offered as a resource and are not intended in any way to be or to imply an endorsement by Thomas Nelson, nor does Thomas Nelson vouch for the existence, content, or services of these sites, phone numbers, companies, or products beyond the life of this book.

ISBN 978-1-4002-3421-9 (HC)
ISBN 978-1-4002-3433-2 (audiobook)
ISBN 978-1-4002-3432-5 (eBook)
ISBN 978-1-4002-3781-4 (IE)

Library of Congress Control Number: 2022935878

Printed in the United States of America

22 23 24 25 26 LSC 10 9 8 7 6 5 4 3 2 1

To my boys,
We are rebuilding this life together.
I am so proud of us.
Love, Mom

CONTENTS

DREAM

LIVE

PROLOGUE

PACKING UP CAMP

If you can't fly then run,
if you can't run then walk,
if you can't walk then crawl,
but whatever you do
you have to keep moving forward.
—MARTIN LUTHER KING JR

I step out of my car and stare at the small single-story home.
It's bright red with white trim, just like a barn. The bottom
half of the home is covered in layered brick with grey mortar
oozing in every direction as if it is melting off the exterior. The
cracked driveway curves around a large front yard filled with
weeds and dirt. The home itself isn't beautiful, but it's nestled

into a charming, historic area of town known as College Park. A neighborhood with wide-open streets shaded by large mature trees and lovely homes dating all the way back to the early 1900s. It is wonderfully idyllic.

I close my eyes. I breathe in. Six months a widow, desperate for respite, chasing down a deep desire to stand on my own two feet—and this place fits within my budget.

Yet, I want to run away from it all.

I feel like an alien in my own life. I want to go back to the warmth of my husband's arms, to the familiarity of a worn-in routine, to the comfort of shared responsibility and deep love, to a life that is safe and predictable. I want to run away from this new world and never look back.

My soul aches. How am I supposed to do this on my own? *God, give me strength.*

Nothing could have prepared me for this new life. My husband Andrew's tragic suicide swiftly swept away every beautiful dream I had for what my life would be. The journey forward has been disorienting. In so many ways, Andrew was my home. So what does *home* look like here? How do I rebuild my life, my family, my future, my home without him? The questions swirl endlessly about my mind as I stand on the uncertain edge of something new. This red barn symbolizes so much more than a home. It's my first baby step toward rebuilding a new life on my own.

I open my eyes; I exhale acceptance. I am here. There is no going back. The ground beneath my feet is where I stand. Forward is the only way to go.

I walk down the driveway, through the white wooden gate, and into the house. Inside, there is a quaint office with a fireplace, a remodeled galley kitchen, a cozy living space with high ceilings and original wood beams, three bedrooms, and two outdated bathrooms. Plenty of room for my three young sons and me. I feel uneasy. The house is beaming with potential, but I am lacking peace. It just doesn't feel right. I leave the home and doubt I'll ever step foot into it again.

Yet, as the days pass, I can't stop thinking about it. My mind begins to paint a powerful picture of the possibilities: white paint covering the exterior, black trim lining the roof, a porch swing swaying just beyond the gate near the front door, fresh landscaping, updated bathrooms, a trampoline, and even a small basketball court in the backyard.

All my daydreaming leads me back through the white wooden gate once more. On this second visit, all the images I painted in my mind come to life. I can see it. I can see us here. Tiny feet running through the halls and pounding on the raised foundation, candles flickering on the fireplace mantel, coffee brewing in the kitchen, the clicks of a keyboard echoing in the office, movie nights with my boys on the couch. The peace I have been searching for is found. I put in an offer, a few weeks later it is accepted, and I am empowered.

I am rebuilding my life, and gratitude pulses through my veins. I know I didn't arrive here alone. Every open door is undeserved grace. God making a way in the wilderness of my pain, gently ushering us into a new place.

On move-in day, I proudly tape David's word from Psalm

34:18 to the front door of my fridge: "The LORD is close to the brokenhearted and saves those who are crushed in spirit." I feel protected, I feel comforted, I feel close to the thin veil. Jehovah-jireh, the Lord will provide: I stand in his beautiful provision, the mystery of life unfolding before my eyes, somehow heartbreak and hope both finding their home in healing.

I pour my heart into that little home, and it shows. The vision becomes reality: white paint, black trim, new bathrooms, updated landscaping, everything I could have ever imagined and more. It is safe, beautiful, and warm; it's home. Yet every time I pull out of the driveway and head into the surrounding cities, those feelings fade as I am brutally reminded of a life that is no longer mine. A life I lived with my husband, who is no longer alive. A life I can never go back to. Memories bombard me everywhere I go. My beautiful home feels like a tent pitched in the cemetery with death surrounding me on all sides.

As much as I love my home, I begin to realize we can't stay. New life can't be built in a cemetery; new life requires new ground. Our little red barn isn't a permanent place but more of a halfway house, a camp, a temporary dwelling place for us to rest, to embrace the reality of death, and to begin dreaming new dreams about a new life.

This realization pours out of my heart and into conversations with friends. As I sit on my front porch swing, gently swaying back and forth, I share these words with my friend Kelsey on the other end of the phone. "I had this beautiful life," I say. "I had everything I could have ever asked for and more, and it's like that whole life died with Andrew and I was handed a brand-new one that I never saw coming. And I so desperately want to believe that this new life, even though it looks really different than before, can still be beautiful too. It's as if I am *rebuilding beautiful*." As those last two words flow from my mouth, I know they are so much bigger than me. I know they carry a powerful message of hope. We don't have to stay camped out in the cemetery. A beautiful world waits for us on the other side of loss. A world so expansive it has room for our pain.

Friend, I have no idea what led you to pick up this book today. Maybe you, too, have experienced deep loss. Perhaps you are walking through the heartbreak of a divorce. Maybe you are in a season of transition after a career change, the death of a dream, or a big move. Whatever your perspective or pain point may be, may this book lead you toward hope. In the pages ahead, I have broken down rebuilding beautiful into five sections—or, as I like to call them, processes: embrace, heal, explore, dream, and live. Through personal stories, Scripture, practical tips, tools, and even an appendix of reflection questions found at the very end of this book, my desire is for us to make discoveries together. We will learn how to embrace our pain, decide to heal, move forward and bravely explore our new world, dare to dream beyond the destruction of a broken reality, and free-fall madly in love with life all over again. Let's start packing up camp. There's so much life ahead!

EMBRACE

(transitive verb): to clasp in the arms; hug, cherish, love[1]

For a while my middle son, Jethro (Jet), was the worst at giving hugs. I would wrap my arms around him, and instead of wrapping his arms around me in return, he would just stand there like a little statue. He is an expert at receiving hugs, but he has been missing out on the joy of the embrace. So we've been practicing. I wrap my arms around him and encourage him to wrap his arms around me too. I squeeze him tight, he squeezes me back, and we share a few laughs. My hope for Jet is that eventually the practice of giving and receiving hugs will become second nature.

When it comes to learning how to embrace our pain, I wonder how many of us are like my sweet Jethro. Slightly uncomfortable, unsure what to do, or perhaps even frozen like a statue. Through these next three chapters, we will dive into what it looks like to stretch our arms out wide, unclench our fists, and embrace the inevitable in a way that is deeply brave, loving, and gracious. We will unpack how to hold space for our pain and also how to invite others into the deeper recesses of our stories and hearts. In this section, I hope to lead us through the pain so we are no longer paralyzed by it. Instead, may we learn to fully participate in the sacred gift that is found in both the lessons of the pain and the new life that waits for us just beyond our darkest days.

CHAPTER 1

EMBRACING THE UNEXPECTED

> Pain nourishes courage. You can't be
> brave if you've only had wonderful things
> happen to you.
> —MARY TYLER MOORE

In the summer of 2014, my husband, Andrew, and I were expecting our second baby boy. Yet the beginning of his life came about in the most unexpected way. As I lay on my back in the wee hours of the morning on the Fourth of July, I was blinded by the blazing fluorescent lights. A stark blue-and-white hospital gown hung loosely over my protruding pregnant belly, and sweat and tears streamed slowly down my face. We weren't supposed to be at the hospital for another six weeks, but pregnancies don't always go according to plan. A healthy newborn baby is truly a precious miracle that involves a multitude of smaller miracles along the way.

While I pushed through the pain of labor, a team of nurses, doctors, and specialists—prepared for the imminent unknown—was ready to rush our newborn son's premature body down the halls and into the healing sanctuary of the neonatal intensive care unit (NICU) the moment he arrived. Andrew stood beside me, a pillar of strength, calm, steadiness, and serenity. His big blue eyes were focused and determined as he leaned in close to whisper, "Everything is going to be okay." Like my mind, the room spun in every direction. *Will it really be okay?*

I closed my eyes as pain and fear flooded my body. Every unsaid expectation I had carefully constructed in my mind crumbled under the heavy weight of reality. This moment didn't belong on the timeline of my life, or my son's life, yet there was no way to stop the inevitable: Our son was coming, and he was coming fast. After one final fiery push he arrived, we named him Jethro (meaning "overflow"), and his presence overflowed our hearts with love.

As the team of doctors had suspected, Jethro's fragile body needed time to heal and grow strong in the NICU. For twenty-seven days our world revolved around a tiny hospital bed where his precious body lay connected to medication and machines supporting his life: a ventilator to help him breathe, a port in his arm to give him medication, a line through his belly button to monitor blood pressure, an IV in his leg to inject blood transfusions, and a urinary catheter to help drain all the fluids being pumped through his little body every day.

All we could do was sit, wait, and pray. It was surreal in every way, as if I was watching someone else's life unfold. This wasn't supposed to happen to us, this wasn't supposed to happen to our son, this wasn't supposed to be a part of our story; yet here we were, living it. Unable to do anything but embrace the unexpected reality set before us.

Friction

Maybe your story doesn't involve a baby in the NICU, but I have a hunch you, too, might be familiar with the jolt of unexpected pain. It wasn't supposed to happen to you, or to your loved one, but it did. Turns out no matter how hard we may try, no one is invincible. We can plan, prepare, and even work tirelessly toward the beautiful life of our dreams, but we can't account for the unexpected. Accidents happen, babies are born early, mental illness strikes, cancer invades, relationships crumble, and careers come to unforeseen ends. It's all part of it: the dark side of life we can't avoid. Each of us is either walking through, headed toward, or just on the other side of a painful human experience. Suffering well and surviving these unexpected encounters depend greatly on our ability to welcome and embrace every one of the painful challenges that comes hurtling our way.

The military world has a phrase for this that I find rather fitting. When faced with extreme situations or unbearable pain, they say the only way forward is to show up, push through, and "embrace the suck." No shortcuts, no ways around it: *Embrace* is the only way through.

Carl von Clausewitz, best known for the influential book *On War*, was the first to loosely introduce this idea of "the suck," which he called "friction."[1] Friction is all of the stuff that gets in the way of our ability to move forward. When we embrace the friction, or "embrace the suck," we aren't ignoring or diminishing our pain; instead, we are stepping toward it with courage. Stepping toward our pain can feel heavy, difficult, scary, or extremely uncomfortable. And stepping toward our pain will almost always cost us something. Maybe it's time, resources, emotional energy, or even physical exertion, but embracing our pain is an action that requires an exchange. This exchange won't feel natural. What *is* natural is our innate desire to unleash our defenses to protect ourselves and our loved ones from pain at all costs.

> No shortcuts, no ways around it: *Embrace* is the only way through.

I'll never forget walking into the NICU for the first time and seeing Jethro hooked up to the oscillator ventilator, a machine described to us by a NICU nurse as "life support for babies." When I turned the corner and saw his chest rapidly rising and falling as the machine pumped oxygen into his lungs, I collapsed, completely unable to control my natural response to this very unnatural circumstance. My reaction was so dramatic that it caught the staff off guard. A nurse even approached me to ask, "Why are you so upset?" Her question was one I couldn't answer because I was still wrapping my mind around this new reality. It all happened so fast.

Our natural reactions to the unexpected may surprise us or even surprise others around us because there is so much more happening beneath the surface. Our minds, our hearts, and our emotions are working hard to catch up to speed with reality. Engaging with our pain, understanding the layers of our trauma, and locating the source of our emotions will take time. There may not be a fast-forward button, but there is always a way through. Sitting next to an incubator holding Jethro's little hand with one finger instead of holding him in my arms wasn't easy. Leaving him at the hospital in order to go home to rest nearly tore my heart in two. To show up fully for that experience, that small blip on the timeline of my life and Jethro's life, took a toll on my mental, emotional, physical, and spiritual health—but I made it through, and so did my sweet Jethro.

Although it may feel uncomfortable, difficult, or even impossible at first, what I've learned as I've engaged with my pain is that when I have welcomed it, embraced it, and worked through it, it has become one of the greatest teachers of my life. Pain changes us. It expands our hearts to make room for empathy and compassion; it loosens our tight grips on all that is fleeting; and it opens our eyes to behold the gift of life that surrounds us every day. To be right here, in this very moment, is a hard-won, precious reward.

Here are a few practices that can help us create space to embrace the sharp edges of our pain and find our way through the unexpected.

1. Don't Run Away

I don't know about you, but I love to run. Running away from my pain and avoiding the hard work of holding space for my broken heart can feel safe. In the middle of the most horrific moments in my life, I've found it difficult to stay in the trenches where the healing happens. The great challenge of our ability to hold a posture of embrace is endurance. How much pain are we willing to take? How deep into the core of our trauma and our wounds are we willing to go? When everything in us wants to run away, how do we develop the strength to stay?

As a student of my own suffering, I still have so much to learn when it comes to embracing my pain. It has brought me great comfort to know that I'm not alone on this journey. I have found solace not only in the redemption stories of others but also in my faith. In Scripture we see that even Jesus was a man well-acquainted with pain. Isaiah 53:3 describes him as a "man of suffering, grief's *patient* friend" (THE VOICE). The final days of his life paint a vivid picture of what it looks like to stay with and surrender to our pain. In Matthew 26:36–46, we are taken to the garden of Gethsemane, where Jesus vulnerably confronted his morality and wrestled deeply with his pain and heartbreak. He was literally on his knees, his face to the ground, begging God to take the pain away. He cried out, "Father, *this is the last thing I want.* If there is any way, please

Pain changes us. It expands our hearts to make room for empathy and compassion; it loosens our tight grips on all that is fleeting; and it opens our eyes to behold the gift of life that surrounds us every day.

take this *bitter* cup from me. Not My will, but Yours be done" (v. 39 THE VOICE).

To stay with the pain may lead us all the way to the edge of ourselves, where everything in us is stretched to the absolute limit. We may find ourselves being led to our own garden of Gethsemane moments: on our knees, our faces to the ground, begging God to take the pain and suffering away. I've had my fair share of these moments; my knees are familiar with the floor. God only knows how many times I've cried out in complete desperation, unsure if I would survive another moment in my daily reality. The truth is, to stay with our pain—and to develop the strength to endure it—is going to hurt like hell. Everything inside of us will want to run away. Our hardwired defenses work tirelessly every day to steer us away from engaging with our pain. So how do we find the peace that Jesus found? How do we arrive at the place where we can say, "Not my will, but yours be done"?

Friend, I'm still walking this long road with you. Life is a constant journey of learning how to let go of the plans I've made in exchange for the plans God has for me. Through time in therapy, reading, prayer, and journaling, I have discovered the importance of taking inventory of my emotions in the middle of these messy moments. Pausing long enough to ask myself: *Am I leaning into my pain, or am I running away?*

As we rebuild our lives and embrace our pain, it can be really easy to let unhealthy habits creep in. If we are escaping our pain through social media, a midday glass of wine, a binge-worthy Netflix show, or extra hours at the office, or if we are even displacing our pain by projecting it onto others, the temporary escape will only delay our forward steps toward the dream of a new kind of beautiful life. If any of these escape outlets sounds familiar to you, maybe it's time to make a change. We can exchange a glass of wine for coffee with a friend, an endless scroll through social media for a helpful book, a Netflix show for a new nighttime routine that relaxes the mind and doesn't keep us wide awake until midnight. Although in the moment it may feel really good to ignore our pain, all we are doing is delaying our healing.

We were never meant to stay stuck in our pain. Even Scripture describes our journey with pain through movement. The psalmist David wrote: "Even though I walk through the darkest valley, I will fear no evil, for you are with me; your rod and your staff, they comfort me" (Psalm 23:4). The valley is no place to make a home. God wants to lead us on a journey *through* the dark valley, toward the light of better days. Pain doesn't have to define our lives, our identities, or our futures. It is when we lean into our pain and ask God to show us how to embrace it that we are transformed. Friend, don't miss out on what your pain wants to teach you. When everything inside of you wants to run away, ask God to fill you with supernatural strength and show you how to stay.

2. Shake Off the Shame

When my husband took his last breath, I took my first as a widow and single mom. The unexpected title of *single mom* has taken some time to sink in, and it has even been a source of shame. To become a single parent, something has to fail or die. Either a relationship, a marriage, a dream, or in my situation, a husband. For a while I wondered if failure was the only thing people could see when they looked at me. I felt like I had failed my husband, failed my children, and even failed myself. I still at times feel an urge to defend myself when I admit to someone new that I'm a single mom. I often follow it by saying: "My husband died, but we're okay." The "my husband died" part is so they don't think this title is something I chose, and the "but we're okay" part is so they don't pity me.

Shame is a powerful weapon that will trap us in pain. Even as I type these words, I have tears streaming down my face. I am still learning how to shake off the shame. I am still learning how to admit that I'm a single mom without giving into the urge to defend myself. To embrace this sharp edge of my story will mean letting go of the strong sense of failure that says I'm a bad person or I did something wrong.

Maybe your shame doesn't stem from single parenting, but perhaps you, too, are familiar with the feeling of failure. Maybe you are on the other side of a failed relationship, medical treatment plan, career, or dream. Maybe you feel like you've failed your spouse, your children, your friends, or even yourself. But the truth is, every time we allow ourselves to settle into the sinkhole of shame, we lose the perspective we need to embrace our pain. To rebuild a beautiful life, we must first shake off the shame so we can engage with our pain in a healthy way. This is a good time to ask ourselves a few questions:

- Why am I feeling shame?
- What external factors are causing it?
- Who can I talk to about it?

As we gain the clarity we need to zoom out and better understand why we are feeling shame, we can begin to welcome our feelings, move through them, and eventually learn to let them go. One of my favorite places to do the letting go is at the ocean. There is a trail where I often go to run that overlooks the salty sea near my home in San Clemente, California. On the really hot days, I love to throw off my shoes at the end of my run and make one final dash straight into the water. It's like a sacred baptism every time as I hold my breath and dive under the waves. It's there at the end of the long, exhausting journey, where I've pushed my body to its limit, that I can finally feel a sense of relief. And as I walk home barefoot with sandy toes and wet clothes, I am reminded that you cannot come up for air until *after* you've jumped right into the murky mess of it all.

Friend, you don't have to drown in your shame for another day. As you show up in this season and ask the hard questions, my hope is that you, too, will come up for air—that all the heaviness you've been carrying around will be washed away as you discover new ways to let go of the burden of shame.

3. Consider Your Future Self

Another way to embrace the unexpected is to think about your future self. For example: It's the end of the day, you finally got the kids to sleep, and you are exhausted, but the house is a complete disaster. Spaghetti is spread all over the table from dinner, in the sink a pile of dirty dishes waits to be washed, the dishwasher still needs to be unloaded, the laundry basket is overflowing, three days' worth of clean clothes wait to be folded and put away, toys are scattered all over the floor, and the trash needs to go out. In this moment you are faced with a decision. Do you turn the light off, crawl into bed, and leave the mess for the morning? Or do you take the next twenty or thirty minutes to dig deep and clean it up?

For me, this is when I ask myself: *What would future Kayla want?* I close my eyes and imagine future Kayla waking up to a clean house, coffee prepped in the coffeepot, laundry folded and ready to be put away, clean dishes in the dishwasher, and an empty sink. Most nights, this vision is the only motivation I need to embrace the mess and clean up the chaos before I head to bed; but this same tactic can be applied to an endless number of circumstances. When we don't want to exercise but show up anyway. When we don't want to read or journal but show up anyway. When we don't want to go to work but show up anyway. When we don't want to share our raw emotions in therapy but show up anyway. When we don't want to embrace our pain but show up anyway. When we show up in this moment, right now, we are also showing up for our future selves. And trust me, your future self will be so grateful for the courage you had to show up today.

When life leads us to an unexpected season or circumstance, we must respond to the unimaginable. Call it an unavoidable opportunity, if you will. Life knocks the wind out of us, and while we are still gasping for air, we ask, "Now what?" This question may be one of the most powerful questions we ever ask ourselves. The way we respond to the "Now what?" will determine how things turn out five years from now.

Friend, you have the power to stand up on your own two feet and fight. You have the power to reframe your reality, to build a new kind of beautiful—perhaps one even more beautiful than the one before. You have the power to let your pain propel you forward or set you back. You have the power to pick up the pen and write the next line of your story. And guess what the best part is? You already have everything you need. As you embrace the unexpected and welcome *what is*, know that you were made for this. Even when the "this" is really hard, you are hardwired to handle it. You are more than capable and can trust yourself to chase every big, beautiful dream and audacious ambition you have. You are the only one who gets to live your life. There is so much more ahead!

CHAPTER 2

CULTIVATING COMMUNITY

Friendship is unnecessary, like philosophy,
like art . . . It has no survival value; rather
it is one of those things which give value to
survival.

—C. S. LEWIS, FROM *THE FOUR LOVES*

Let's jump right in to this raw truth: We were never designed
to carry our pain alone. Period. End of story. No ifs, ands,
or buts. Whether we believe it or not, hands are reaching out
to share in our suffering, to carry the weight of the burden,
and to lighten the load. It is when we grasp these hope-filled
hands that healing begins. The pain we carry for others is not a

burden. To be invited into the pain of another is a sacred honor. Although at first we may feel as if we are weighing down conversations with our heavy hearts, what I've come to discover is that we won't be alone for long. Life has a way of handing each of us our own prescription for pain. The gift we receive when others share in our suffering is the same beautiful gift we will be able to return one day.

> To be invited into the pain of another is a sacred honor.

Some of my deepest friendships began in the fall of 2007 when my shaky feet first stepped onto the campus of Vanguard University, a small private Christian college in Southern California. I welcomed a fresh start in a place where I knew no one and no one knew me, where the opportunities were endless and overwhelming. This was my Independence Day, my once-in-a-lifetime opportunity to create something on my own, away from home. I gave my mom a hug and told her goodbye as I headed to the dorms to settle in. The dorm room was large, and the sun peaked through the tinted window, offering a small amount of light to the shaded space. There were two sets of bunk beds, but I had only been assigned one roommate—a transfer student who didn't seem at all interested in making new friends. After a brief introduction, she dropped off her belongings and left me all alone. Just three empty beds, a few Home Depot boxes, and me. My big beautiful expectations collided with a surprising reality, and I was utterly disappointed. I wondered, *Is this what my college experience will be?*

I pulled myself together and headed downstairs to the

freshman orientation kickoff. The campus was buzzing; noise and music filled the atmosphere as students arrived. There were people cheering, shouting, and waving banners and signs; older students were welcoming new students; and families were holding back tears as they said their final goodbyes. As I wandered around the campus searching for a place to belong, I felt a deep sense of solidarity for the first time. As it turned out, I wasn't alone after all; there were hundreds of new students with big dreams and nervous grins searching for connection too. I found my assigned orientation group, a small circle of other freshmen the school had randomly bunched together, and plopped down on the grass. Sitting next to me was a girl with a friendly smile and long, blond, curly hair. Her name was Alicia, and she became my first college friend.

Alicia quickly took me under her wing, introduced me to all her new friends, and helped me see that the school had made a big mistake with my dorm room assignment. Somehow, I had ended up in the dormitory reserved for sophomores and transfers instead of the freshman dorm. After a few quick conversations with the residential staff, I was given the green light to move into a room just across the hall from Alicia. In a flash I went from alone in an empty dorm to immersed in community. This pivotal moment shifted my entire college experience. From that day forward, college became everything I had imagined and more: late-night shenanigans at the local Denny's, road trips with friends up the coast, all-nighters spent cramming for exams, sunset surfing at the beach, crushes on boys, and guitar jam sessions in the lobby. A magical college freshman experience where lifelong friendships were born.

Eleven years later, when I found myself standing at the edge of another brand-new life, those same friends surrounded me once again. We were able to pick up right where we left off. At first it was obvious that our time together was just for me—to make me feel loved, seen, and held in a tender season. But as the months passed, I realized our time together was really for all of us. Our monthly dinners have become a sacred space where we can vulnerably pour out our pain, our hopes, our dreams, our doubts, and our desires. A space where belly laughs and ugly cries are both deeply felt and welcomed. A space where no topic is off the table, where we laugh until we cry, where we cry until we laugh, and where our pain truly is shared and lifted. As I have slowly embraced my new reality, these friends have walked with me, loved me, cared for me, and carved out time to simply be with me—and I have had the honor of doing the same for them.

One of our favorite places to be together is a quaint Italian restaurant called Mama D's in Newport Beach, California. Over wine and piles of pasta with pink sauce, we have shared this season of our lives. From grieving the loss of my husband, to celebrating new business ventures, to processing a Down syndrome diagnosis during a pregnancy, to grieving the death of a father, to sharing in the ups and downs of parenting, dating, and marriage—I cherish these nights with my precious friends. Their deep love and genuine friendship have taught me that rebuilding beautiful isn't a solo endeavor; it's something we do together.

The Gift of Solidarity

My friends from college aren't the only people who have walked alongside me in this new life. When my husband took his last breath, I joined a brave club of fierce women who have also lost their husbands. The story of Andrew's death struck a chord with people all around the world, which gifted me the unique opportunity to connect with others who shared a similar loss. Just a few days into my journey as a widow, I was able to pick up the phone and call another widow named Brittany who was also a young mom of three boys. She was just a few years ahead of me on the grief journey, but talking to Brittany on the phone gave me hope that my kids and I would be okay. I thought to myself, *If she can survive this, then I can survive this too.*

As a single woman and mom, I feel some painfully lonely moments. Bedtimes, mealtimes, weekends, and the sidelines of my sons' sports are just a few of the times when I think of my fellow widow friends the most. In these moments I can close my eyes and remember that there are people like Brittany, and like me, scattered all around the world, bravely showing up and pushing through pain too. The powerful gift of solidarity is accessible to anyone; we can tap into it anywhere, at any time.

Friend, you may feel like you are all alone in the depths of your pain, but you're not. An army of fellow fighters is also digging their heels in, refusing to give up on dreams of a new kind of beautiful life. If you are walking through the loss of a child, know there are other families walking through the same loss. If you are walking through the loss of a marriage, know you aren't the only one picking up the pieces. If you are walking through the death of a dream, know there are thousands of other dreamers out there who are grieving with you. If you are facing a diagnosis you never saw coming, know you and your loved ones aren't the only ones receiving bad news. Although your loss or circumstance may feel unique, remember that around the world—possibly even in your own neighborhood—people are courageously walking down a similar path, wondering how the world keeps spinning while their life is changed forever. Find these people. Find the fellow warriors. Find a community that sees you and understands you at a depth no one else will ever be able to reach. Solidarity is powerful, and it is available to you.

Ruth and Naomi

One of my favorite stories of the power of solidarity is that of Ruth and Naomi. If you've read the book of Ruth, you might be familiar with this tale of two women: a mother-in-law and her daughter-in-law, both unexpected widows, who fought hard to find their way forward after a series of horrific tragedies.

Following the death of her husband and sons, Naomi decided to make the long journey back to her native home. She tried to convince both Ruth and her other daughter-in-law to let her go alone, urging them to stay in their own country with their own belief system. Naomi argued her daughters-in-law were young enough to possibly marry again one day. But Ruth refused to leave

Naomi's side, and in doing so chose to walk away from everything she knew. "Don't force me to leave you," Ruth said. "Don't make me go home. Where you go, I go; and where you live, I'll live. Your people are my people, your God is my god; where you die, I'll die, and that's where I'll be buried, so help me GOD—not even death itself is going to come between us!" (Ruth 1:16–17 MSG).

Ruth's words are piercing in this heartrending moment of the story. Were it a scene in a movie, I can imagine the score playing in the background, the buildup, the tension, and the emotion of this pivotal exchange. Ruth made a life-altering decision to be with Naomi. Not only that, but because of the strong cultural divides at this time in history, Ruth knew she would be considered an outsider, an outcast, or even an enemy of society if she went with Naomi—but she was willing to go anyway. Those of us whose culture values and praises independence may see this as an extreme choice. As I read this story I couldn't help but wonder: *Why? Why would Ruth ever choose to sacrifice herself like that?* The only answer I could find is love. Because she loved her mother-in-law too much to let her suffer alone. This is the kind of solidarity that takes your breath away. Powerful, moving, rare, unbelievable, sacrificial love.

Later on in the story, we see redemption for both Ruth and Naomi. Ruth met and found favor with a kind and generous man named Boaz, who looked out for her, let her glean his fields, and even provided extra food for her to take home to Naomi. As she began to see God's hand writing a new kind of beautiful story, Naomi said: "GOD hasn't quite walked out on us after all! He still loves us, in bad times as well as good!" (Ruth 2:20 MSG).

Solidarity, faithfulness, love, friendship, and redemption: It's the formula for a really great story, one we could read over and over again. Not only are we reminded of the power of solidarity through the story of Ruth and Naomi, but we are also reminded of the goodness of God. Although we might not see our circumstances as good right now, like Ruth, we can choose to stay faithful, to work hard, to love sacrificially, and to fight for a way forward even when the path looks grim. May we all strive to be as good of a friend as Ruth was to Naomi. May we all strive to find the solidarity they found.

Perhaps the key to surviving, thriving, and encountering God's love in a circumstance we never saw coming is through people—the people who would love nothing more than to be invited into the messy, level-zero rebuilding process with us.

Just a year after my first phone call with Brittany, I found myself on the receiving end of a similar phone call. A brand-new widow daunted by an unforeseen future and overwhelmed by grief called me looking for the same reassurance that I had once needed. I can confidently say my answer to her was the same answer I would give to anyone sitting across the table from me today: It will be okay. I don't know *how* it will, I don't know *who* it will involve, but I know there is always a way through to okay. Maybe even better than okay, perhaps even more beautiful than we imagined *okay* could ever be. I'm not there yet, but I haven't lost hope that *better than okay* is still waiting in the future for me.

> I know there is always a way through to okay.

Ways to Connect with Others

To rebuild beautiful in our lives, we need our own Ruths and Naomis; we need to search for the life-giving gift of solidarity. We need to embrace others and allow others to embrace us too. We can choose to pick up the phone and finally reach out to that person who is a few years ahead of us on the rebuilding journey. We can choose to say yes to a night out with friends, away from our unrelenting responsibilities at home. We can choose connection over isolation and healing over hiding in our pain. Friend, if you don't know where to start, here are a few simple ways to connect with others and share the heavy burden of your pain.

Social Media

Social media can be overwhelming, loud, and messy, but it can also be a beautiful place for connection. It was through the Instagram platform that I reached out for the first time to another young widow. I sent her this direct message: "Hi, I don't know your story, but I know you also lost your husband unexpectedly at a young age with young children. I just lost my husband last night after he attempted to take his own life on Friday morning. I have three young boys and I am so devasted I don't know what to do." She messaged me back later that day with some encouragement, her phone number, and five powerful words: "I am here for you."

Sending that direct message gave me access to a relationship with someone whom I would have otherwise never connected with. It may feel totally out of your comfort zone to hit send on a message like that, but the risk is worth the reward. There are really kind people in the world who would love nothing more than to share in your pain and say those same five words to you: "I am here for you."

Groups

Seeking out a local group is another way to connect with others who are walking through a similar season or suffering a similar loss. A simple Google search can direct you to groups like GriefShare, DivorceCare, Celebrate Recovery, or niche groups that are more specific to your unique loss. There are even online community platforms that host spaces like this virtually, so you can find connection in the comfort of your own home. The heartbeat of these spaces is simple: You are not alone, and you don't have to carry your pain on your own for another day.

A little less than a year after my husband died, I stepped into a space like this for the first time. I traveled across the country to the white sandy shores of Alys Beach, Florida, to meet with a group called Never Alone Widows. The hosts of the group welcomed each of us by name and with a warm embrace—the kind of embrace that whispers "I see you" without saying a word. We met in a stunning three-story beach house overlooking the ocean and spent the weekend holding space for each other's pain. We shared our stories out loud, we gleaned wisdom from a panel of women who had walked the road before us, we prayed for one another, and we even dressed up for a fancy dinner to celebrate the gift of togetherness. The shift in the atmosphere over those three days of fellowship was tangible. Many of us had stepped into the room heavy, defeated, and exhausted, yet we walked away feeling lighter, refreshed, and full of hope. Since that very first group experience, I have been honored to serve other widows alongside the Never Alone Widows team through encounters just like this. Doing so has truly been one of my greatest joys.

Lifelines

As we learn to invite others into the depths of our healing and rebuilding process, we give buoyancy to the weight of our pain. Although a vast sea of grief, loss, and uncertainty threatens to drown us completely, we can choose to reach out for the lifelines being thrown our way. These lifelines of love from family, friends, therapists, and others who are bereaved sustain us with the strength and hope needed to ride out our darkest days.

Not only are we held safely in the arms of others who are shouldering the weight of our circumstance, we are held even more securely in the steady love of God. When we tap into this everlasting love in the midst of our profound suffering, we find that God is still whispering peace. Even here, in the middle of the unknown, in the questions, in the heartache, and in the depths of our deepest pain, we encounter an indescribable peace holding us close. As we embrace every sharp edge of this season of life, may we choose to let God and let others embrace it with us. We were never meant to carry our pain alone. Together is how we find a way forward. One brave day at a time.

CHAPTER 3

BEFRIENDING DEATH

One who does not embrace death will not
know life at all.

—SADHGURU

I was ten years old when my dad took me driving for the first
time. I climbed onto the bench seat of his well-worn white two-
door truck, and we headed south to the abandoned dairy roads a
few towns away—just him and me. When we found a safe place
to stop, my dad invited me to slide over from the passenger's seat
to sit on his lap. My eyes filled with wonder; my big moment had
arrived. I clenched the black leather steering wheel as my dad
gently pushed on the gas, and we were off. An exhilarating rush

of adrenaline filled my body as I took in the view from the driver's seat for the very first time. I felt powerful behind the wheel: a small taste of freedom, a glimpse into a future world waiting for me. One day my legs would be long enough to reach the pedals below. One day I'd be old enough to take the wheel and go wherever I wanted to go.

Then, as life would have it, that day came. I grew up, got my license, left home, went to college, fell in love, and got married—yet somehow, as my husband took the steering wheel of our lives, I found myself metaphorically sitting in the passenger seat all over again. Most days I didn't mind my view from the passenger's seat; I was grateful for our predictable and stable life. We were doing meaningful work within our ministry at the church, and I was soaking up extra time with our three sons as a stay-at-home mom. Then nearly eight years into building a life together, everything changed. Andrew was gone, and life invited me to slide into the driver's seat once again. This time as an adult with a heavy burden of responsibility, a heart full of grief, an abyss of possibilities expanding across the horizon, and three precious boys shouting from the back row, "Mommy, where are we going next?"

The Unknown

The road ahead isn't always clear. During our brief time here, some seasons will lead us into the unknown. The unknown can look different for everybody. For me, I've encountered the unknown in life after loss. Perhaps it's the same for you, or maybe you've experienced the death of a dream, a relationship, a marriage, or even a job. Your predictable course went off the rails, and you've found yourself staring out over an endless, intriguing, yet terrifying abyss.

This is where things get interesting. The way I see it, we have two options: We can choose to let go of *what was* and embrace the unknown of *what is*, or we can cling to a life that's no longer viable. Option one invites new life to begin where the old life ended, while option two entraps us in one long, drawn-out death. Life never really begins again if we hold fast to what can no longer be. If we think back on the prologue of this book, we could say option two keeps us "camped out in the cemetery"— alive but surrounded by death. To rebuild beautiful, it's essential to embrace death as a pathway to new life.

Embracing Physical Death

We often avoid things that make us uncomfortable, and for many of us, death is at the top of that list. Many Westerners have especially lost touch with the rituals of death, and for some the topic of death is often private or hidden.

I've been around the mystery of a deceased human body only twice in my life. Once at a wake, and a second time in the hospital room as I watched my husband exhale his last breath. Although the circumstances of both situations were vastly different, my response was the same. I was highly emotional and extremely uncomfortable. The emptiness of my loved one's body was too painful to witness, and everything inside of me wanted to bolt out of the room. Maybe I have a slight case of necrophobia, or perhaps I may feel disconnected from death because no one ever taught me how to embrace it.

Conversations surrounding death are often considered "morbid," so we tend to evade the topic completely. Just last night I was sitting on the sidelines of my son's soccer game, and right beside me was another mom I had just met. In between cheering on our sons, we were engaging in some small talk. Prior to Andrew's death, I didn't mind small talk, as it came with the territory of being a pastor's wife. These days, it's something I've come to abhor. At first this new mom and I exchanged the usual: "How many kids do you have? Where do your kids go to school? How long have you lived in town?" Then came the kicker.

Soccer mom: "How about your husband? Where's he?"
Me: "He actually passed away, so it's just me."
Soccer mom: "Oh, I'm sorry about your husband."
Me: "Thanks."

End of conversation.

This is a prime example of how we avoid talking about death in America. We often don't know how to respond, so we quickly move on to talk about something more pleasant. There are so many follow-up questions the soccer mom could have asked me in that moment. For example: "How did he die? How long has he been gone? How are you holding up without him? How are your kids holding up?" But instead she turned to the woman sitting next to her and asked, "So, how was your vacation?"

Now, I'm not here to shame a soccer mom. She was so sweet and totally caught off guard by my answer to her question. The point I'm getting at is that she, like many of us, has learned how to dance around death as if it doesn't exist. Sadly, if we spend our whole lives dancing around death instead of learning how to embrace it, we will miss a significant piece of life's essence.

> If we spend our whole lives dancing around death instead of learning how to embrace it, we will miss a significant piece of life's essence.

Ways to Befriend Death

From the moment we are born, life is one long farewell. We are all learning how to die. When we embrace this reality we learn how to appreciate the beauty of life without clinging to it. It's all "here today and gone tomorrow" (Job 4:20 MSG). Our experience with loss should change us. Loss should change the way we see, the way we surrender, and ultimately, the way we live. To experience tragedy and move through life unchanged would be an even greater defeat. As we learn to befriend the subject of death, here are some of the ways we can lean in.

1. Engage the Conversation

Perhaps the first step toward embracing death is simply creating space for vulnerable conversations about it. Just last week as I was out to dinner with my friends, the topic of death came up. Instead of shying away from the subject, we went around the table and each took a turn sharing about the fears we have surrounding death. It was a raw and emotional conversation, and many of us were speaking our true fears aloud for the very first time. Was it uncomfortable for some? Absolutely. But the gift we receive through embracing death and engaging in conversations like this now is a heart more prepared to welcome the reality of death when it comes.

2. Prepare Now for the End of Life

When Andrew was alive, we hardly ever talked about death. When the topic did come up, he usually joked about how he was going to die first. We were young and naïve enough to think that death was something we would deal with decades down the road. But then, when he died just a few months after his thirtieth birthday, our family was utterly unprepared. We were forced to plan his memorial service without any of his input. The songs we sang, the plot we chose at the cemetery, and even the suit we sent to the mortuary for his burial were decisions we made without him. This experience has opened my eyes to the importance of considering my own death now. Where do I want to be laid to rest? What songs, verses, poems, or letters do I want my loved ones to read? How do I want my family to respond to my death? One of the most loving things you can do for your family is to answer some of these questions now so that no one is left filling in the blanks when you die. If this is something that's important to you, write it all down—every last detail—and then tuck it away in a special place where your loved ones will know to find it.

3. Hold Space for the Uncomfortable

If talking about death or preparing for your own death is uncomfortable, then holding space for the bereaved is most likely uncomfortable too. Many of us have failed miserably to "mourn with those who mourn" (Rom. 12:15). Oftentimes we don't know what to say, or we disengage completely out of fear of saying the wrong thing. Perhaps the best thing we can do is to shift our focus from showing up with an agenda to simply showing up with love. Here are some words we can always use: "I don't know what to say, but I'm right here, and I love you."

I was fresh in my journey with grief when one of my closest friends came to my home to spend the afternoon with me and my boys. At the end of the day, after I finally got all three of my sons to sleep, I walked out into the living room and collapsed on the floor. As I loudly wept and cried out in pain, my friend curled up beside me, wrapped her arms around me, and wept too. She didn't try to manipulate the moment, she didn't try to find the perfect words, and she didn't try to make me feel better or take away my pain; she simply held me and shared in my suffering. Although she may have felt uncomfortable or unsure of what to do, her loving presence spoke volumes.

Welcoming *What Is*

Death is just one of the many losses we will embrace over time. Each death we face will inevitably lead us to a threshold, a place of transition where we must move forward from the life that once was and welcome the reality of *what is*. Yes, death is absolutely an end, but even more importantly, it is also a new beginning. Psychologists call this stage of welcoming "acceptance." When we have truly found acceptance, we have welcomed *what is* and stopped fighting to hold onto *what was*. We let go of our desire for control, we release our need to understand it all, and we bravely choose hope—to "expect with confidence" that a beautiful life is waiting in the future for us.

However, stepping into a new life doesn't mean leaving the pain behind. Instead the pain moves forward with us, becoming a sacred part of who we are now. Our pain has granted us access to a deeper stream of humanity. We may have been naïve before, but now we are awakened to the paradox of existence. Life is both beautiful and terrible, wonderful and horrible, meaningful and mysterious—all tangled and twisted together.

At six years old, just months after his dad passed away, my son Smith articulated this paradox perfectly. It was Mother's Day 2019, my first Mother's Day as a widow. The school my boys attended invited each of the kindergarten moms to join the class for a "Mother's Day Makeover." We grabbed our mirrors, makeup bags, hair spray, and scrunchies, then found our way into the colorful classroom. The moms sat on little chairs and let little hands make a wonderful mess of our faces. Once our

Life is both beautiful and terrible, wonderful and horrible, meaningful and mysterious—all tangled and twisted together.

"makeovers" were over, the kids proudly handed us our gifts. Sandwiched in between stick figure drawings, handmade cards, and over-the-top crafts was one of those Mother's Day fill-in-the-blank forms—the kind where our kids list out facts about our age, our favorite food, our favorite hobbies, etc. As I sat on that little chair and read that silly little list, one particular line gutted me: "I love it when my mom takes me to *the cemetery* and *Disneyland*." Literally the saddest place on earth and the happiest place on earth in the same sentence. In those blanks sat everything true about our life.

Moving forward after tragedy is finding solidarity with the mysteries of life and death. We find a way to live *happysad*. My three sons and I will be sad that Andrew died for the rest of our lives, but we can still choose to be happy. It's a daily choice to welcome and acknowledge the pain, and it's a daily choice to welcome and chase the joy.

Wounds Are Sacred

The wounds we carry with us are not obstacles to simply get over. Rather, our wounds are the way *through*. Our wounds aren't something to hide or deny; instead, they are sacred parts of who we are and testaments of our journeys. At first, we may not have eyes to see our loss as a gift—how could it be?—because it's too painful. But as we sit with our suffering and courageously welcome and move through our loss, we are transformed. Loss gives us new eyes to see the grace threaded through all humanity.

Our wounds are not separate, but a sacred part of the gift of life. Through our wounds, we are empowered to offer healing to others in pain. Compassion is born in the heart of the wounded. The Latin root of the word *compassion* is *compati*, which literally means to "suffer with one."[1] We can only truly suffer with those who are suffering once we have endured suffering ourselves.

> Compassion is born in the heart of the wounded.

We see this same pattern of sacred woundedness weaved throughout the story of Jesus. Jesus wasn't a savior unacquainted with suffering; he was "a man who suffered, who knew pain firsthand" (Isa. 53:3 MSG). And it is "by his wounds we are healed" (Isa. 53:5). He is the ultimate wounded healer. To experience our own suffering is to partake not only in the suffering of humanity but also in the suffering of our Savior.

Here is where the hope comes in. If we follow the way of Jesus, we know sorrow and suffering are not the end of the story. We live in the light of the resurrection. Yes, Jesus suffered greatly, but he rose again. And to believe in the resurrection is to believe we, too, will rise. Death is no longer an enemy to be feared because we have hope beyond the grave. This hope is a "sure and steadfast anchor of the soul" (Heb. 6:19 ESV). When tragedy strikes, when death feels like it's won, when we've hit rock bottom and can't see a way to live with the pain for another day, hope is the way through.

The pain we are facing today doesn't exempt us from future pain. The road ahead will most likely take unexpected twists and turns, but as we grasp the steering wheel, shift the car into drive, and bravely begin paving a new way through, we can rest assured that we are not navigating the unknown alone. Just like that day on the old dairy roads when I sat safely in my father's arms, we are held right here too. Hope is the vehicle that drives us forward, and divine love is the safety belt holding us secure.

HEAL

(transitive verb): to make free from injury or disease; to make sound or whole; to make well again; to restore to health[1]

I recently decided it was time to remodel the outdated master bathroom in our home. It had a shower full of chipped tile, a faucet that only spewed out scalding hot water, warped laminate flooring, and rusted cast-iron plumbing that leaked into the crawl space under our home. Confident and ambitious, I handed each of my sons a hammer, and we started ripping the bathroom apart. Three days later, hands covered in Band-Aids, house layered in dust, and one massive pile of debris in the driveway, the demolition was finished. The studs were exposed, the plywood floor was bare, and it was time to start building something new.

I innocently believed I could complete the entire project in a week. I mean, it was just a bathroom; how hard could it be? Well, as it turns out, pretty dang hard. The process was slow and messy, and the learning curve was steep. Mortar everywhere, hands cracked and bleeding—exhausting and backbreaking days.

As I worked on the remodel every day, I couldn't help but think about how rebuilding a bathroom is much like rebuilding a life. After all the damage is done and we feel a little naked, vulnerable, and empty, it takes time and immense effort to make something beautiful again. The truth is, beneath every beautiful bathroom are hours of unseen labor. To rebuild a beautiful life, we have to be willing to show up for the hard work of healing. That's what this next section is all about: the unseen. In the next three chapters, we will explore what it looks like to reclaim our identities, write new narratives, and show up for the work of inner healing.

CHAPTER 4

WHO AM I?

Be yourself; everyone else is already taken.
—Unknown

After I survived the first momentous year of loss, I mustered up the courage to finally sort through boxes and bags of Andrew's clothes. I had already cleared the items from the closets after he died so the atmosphere of our house would match the heartbreaking message I shared with my boys: "Daddy isn't coming home." The boys were only two, four, and five years old when their daddy died, so I worried that if they walked into our home and saw his clothes hanging in the closet, his shoes stacked in the garage, or even his truck parked in the driveway, the hope of a grand return would rise up in their little hearts and crush them all over again. I needed the message to be loud and clear—not only for their hearts, but for mine too.

As I sat on the floor and sorted through his belongings, the sharp pain of my reality came rushing to the surface of my mind. A red flannel shirt, the shirt he picked out for our last date night together. Twenty-five pairs of shoes because shoes were his thing. A thin striped button-down shirt, the special one he proudly wore on our wedding day. A large stack of board shorts, his favorite things to wear all summer. The memories were scattered all over my floor, and my heart shattered into a million pieces all over again. I whispered through tears, "He should be here."

Sorting through Andrew's clothes and choosing what should stay and what should go is such a metaphor for my life. As my broken heart begins to heal and I learn to embrace the truth of his not being here—*that he isn't coming home*—I've learned that I, too, must decide what stays and what goes. What parts of me died with Andrew? Who am I now that he's gone? Who do I want to become?

Maybe these questions sound familiar. As you sorted through your own brokenness, have you wondered: *What stays and what goes?* What parts of yourself died with that relationship, marriage, career, or life transition? What will you choose to leave behind? What parts of who you were in your past life no longer serve you in your present? As you look toward the future, what new dreams or aspirations are being birthed within your heart? Who are you becoming? As we say goodbye to the life that once was and welcome the reality of *what is*, we have the opportunity to choose what we take forward with us. We get to decide who we want to be.

The Journey Inward

My beloved role as wife was and still is one of the greatest honors of my life. I have so much admiration and respect for who Andrew was and the beautiful parts of him that are still alive in me and our children. He was one of my greatest teachers. I gleaned so much wisdom just from being by his side. He worked tirelessly to create a beautiful life for our family. I loved being wrapped up in everything he was. But, if I'm being honest, I was so wrapped up in the relationship that I lost my sense of self. I sometimes felt very small and insignificant in the shadow of my husband. I can see clearly now that there was a stark power imbalance in our relationship that wasn't healthy. I found my purpose and identity in supporting his needs, often at the cost of my own.

When Andrew died, in a cruel and upside-down way, I was set free. For the first time in years I could put my own needs first. Right away, I enrolled all three of my boys in full-time school, giving them the gift of a daily routine in a safe and loving community, while also giving myself the gift of space and time—time I needed to grieve, breathe, take a good look in the mirror, and get to know myself all over again. I had to ask myself: *If I'm no longer Andrew's wife, then who am I now?* Similar questions are some of the most painful ones we may encounter in our journey of rebuilding, because an identity crisis is no small issue. When a role, career, or relationship that gave meaning and purpose to us ends, we may struggle to find the strength, courage, or passion to begin again.

The daunting task of reclaiming identity is really a journey inward. It's digging deep to discover who we were each uniquely created to be. For me, the journey inward has felt like resurrection; for a while I forgot who I was, and it took a death to wake me up to life. As the parts of me that lay dormant for years reawakened, I started making a list of the moments when I felt most alive. On my little list I wrote: "running, paddleboarding, spending time with friends, reading, writing, surfing, cooking, traveling alone, traveling with my kids, being spontaneous, lighthearted TV shows, going to bed early, saying yes more than saying no, house projects, power tools, road trips . . ."

As you awaken to who you are now and step toward who you'd like to become, perhaps it's time to start making your own list. Write down all the things that bring you joy. When do you feel most alive? What hobbies have you left behind that you'd like to pick up again? What new passions do you want to pursue?

Reclaiming your identity isn't some New Age or self-help voyage toward "becoming the best version of yourself." Instead it's simply about dying to the *false* self—the version of yourself that you may have created for survival but never really felt like home. Have you lost track of who God made you to be? I believe he is beckoning us to let go of our falsified selves, our deep longing to be approved of by others, and our tendencies to define ourselves by successes, achievements, or accolades. It's

When a role, career, or relationship that gave meaning and purpose to us ends, we may struggle to find the strength, courage, or passion to begin again.

in the safety of his love that we are finally free. No more striving. No more climbing the ladder of success only to discover it's lonely and empty at the top. No more stretching ourselves thin to prove we deserve joy. No more exhausting ourselves through extra hours at the office or deriving our value from likes on Instagram. To be fully known and loved—to be fully free to step into who we were created to be—is to return home to the love that has encircled us all along. This love, God's love, has been there and will be there no matter how far away from it we stray.

I find great comfort in a parable Jesus told: that of the prodigal son. The prodigal son is all of us. We get a little lost sometimes, a little tangled and twisted up in the pressures of daily life. We lose sight of where we are going and wind up far from home. In this story, a son cashed out early on his inheritance and left the afety of his father's home to see what the world had to offer. After squandering his wealth and coming up empty on his search to be loved by the world, he returned home empty-handed. And as the story goes, "while he was still a long way off, his father saw him and was filled with compassion for him; he ran to his son, threw his arms around him and kissed him" (Luke 15:20). The father could have chosen anger, resentment, or rejection, but instead he chose love. He not only chose love, but he also chose to show it by throwing a big party to celebrate his son's return.

Maybe you feel like your circumstances are your fault. Maybe you're trapped in a pit of "could have, would have, should have." Maybe you'd be the first to admit you arrived in this season of rebuilding through a series of poor life choices.

Maybe you feel not only lost in your identity but also un-deserving of love. Friend, there is a Father waiting with open arms to welcome you home. You are beloved. You are deserving of a beautiful life. Healing and hope are waiting for you. Your past doesn't have to define your future. You get to choose who you want to become.

I am learning that it may take a lifetime to answer the ques-tion of who I am. Perhaps it's because the answer is ever-changing. There are many versions of myself that have shaped me into the person I am today, and the person I am today is actively shaping the version of myself I've yet to meet. But the wild joy of it all is that I get to be right here. I get to show up today *just as I am*. I get to love my three sons *just as they are*. I get to step in and out of a hundred different versions of myself. I get to try, try, and try again, knowing I haven't yet arrived and am never fully finished. The process is an endless return to love. It's an endless return to the Father's open arms. It's living daily with unclenched hands, knowing that life is a fleeting, precious gift.

Who Do I Want to Become?

That red flannel I encountered as I sorted through Andrew's clothes made its way into my closet. It's become a staple of my wardrobe. When most people see me wearing it, they have no idea what it represents. Somehow that red flannel makes me feel close to Andrew. When I was deciding what should stay and what should go, I simply couldn't part with it. Every time I reach for the red flannel, I am reminded of him. As I wear it here in this new life, I am reminded of his love that lives here too. The mystery of love is that it doesn't die; love is what we leave behind.

As I reflect on who I want to become, the answer is simply a person of love. If love is the gift I can leave behind, then how can I embody it fully in this one lifetime? I'm still learning how to answer this question. I am still growing in my ability to love others freely and deeply. I am still learning how to tame my own ego, which is desperate for affection and attention. May these desires no longer distract me from seeing and loving others well.

To become a person of love is to become like the father in the story of the prodigal son. We are all invited to the celebration. We are all invited to live differently during our short time here. We are all invited to tap into the intimate well of his expansive love. We are all invited to share in his joy. The questions, then, are: Will we accept the invitation? Will we stop clinging to all the shallow things we think define us? What will it take for love to be the loudest message we live?

> What will it take for love to be the loudest message we live?

To step toward this kind of love takes great discipline—an awareness of the thousands of little choices we make every day. In this season of rebuilding, we can choose to live in the sorrow of our circumstances—where loss defines us, where we believe we "deserve" to be bitter, sad, or mad at the world. Or we can choose to accept the invitation to rebuild a new kind of beautiful life. A life built on a firm foundation of love will never die. We do not have to deny the pain, but we can choose not to live in it. May we be set free to step into the fullness of who we were uniquely created to be. Friend, the choice is yours. Be brave. Be gentle. Live in grace. You are safe, you are loved, and you have nothing to prove. You get to choose who you want to become.

CHAPTER 5

A NEW NARRATIVE

What we have once enjoyed we can never
lose . . . All that we love deeply becomes a
part of us.

—HELEN KELLER

It was the summer of 2020. The world had been shut down for
around four months, and after strictly following the locally
enforced social distancing and stay-at-home orders, it was time
for my cooped-up boys and me to break out of the house.

Air travel felt uncertain and unsafe with a novel coronavirus
unleashed in the world, so we decided to head out on an adventure
in our SUV. The road trip would begin at our home in Southern

California and end at our friends' home in Northern Idaho. The journey would take at least twenty hours, which meant two solid days in the car. After studying the map, I decided a good half-way point to stop and rest for the night would be in the beautiful resort town of Park City, Utah.

As I looked over our itinerary, I realized our visit to Park City would fall on Father's Day—a day that is deeply painful every year. It starts with Father's Day crafts at school, usually created in the last days of the school year. Then the giant Father's Day banners in every big-box store, followed by the countless commercials on almost every media outlet showcasing dads and their families happily celebrating a special day together. Hallmark holidays are unavoidable, and as much as I wish I could magically make the day disappear, I just can't. But what I can do is change the narrative. The day will always be difficult, but maybe there's a way to make it beautiful too.

As I thought about our time in Park City and how I could make that Father's Day special, a lightbulb sparked in my mind. Park City just so happened to be the last place Andrew and I visited together when he was alive, and my favorite memory from that trip was the day we spent off-roading through the mountains on a dune buggy. I called it "Andrew's adventure day," and it was one of the best days we ever had together. It's a memory I will cherish forever. So, I decided I would take the boys on their own dune buggy adventure to the same place Andrew took me. Together we would embrace the really terrible day but also make beautiful new memories by doing something their daddy loved to do.

We hit the road early Saturday morning and drove all day through California, Nevada, Arizona, and Utah, finally arriving at our pit stop in Park City. After resting for the night at our hotel, we woke up Sunday morning full of joy and anticipation for our big Father's Day adventure. The dune buggy sat lifted high off the ground, complete with giant tires, a roll cage, and four big bucket seats. The boys' eyes opened wide with wonder as we climbed into the off-roading machine. My youngest son, Brave, sat proudly in the front passenger's seat next to me, while the two older boys sat strapped in the back. We buckled our seatbelts, took a quick look at the printed map, and were off!

The dune buggy purred loudly as we drove on the dirt road up the mountainside. We spent the next few hours having an absolute blast zipping through mud puddles, swerving between tall trees, and taking in the majesty and beauty with all our senses. Toward the end of our journey we stopped at an outlook perched at the very top of the mountain—the same place where Andrew and I had stopped together to take a picture just a few years earlier.

I found a secure spot to capture the moment with my phone camera, hit the self-timer button, and ran to join the boys on top of the dune buggy. I laughed while the boys did "the dab," and we all threw our hands in the air. We were creating a new narrative, and the moment was filled with the pure joy and freedom of redemption. Instead of sulking in the sadness, we were laughing and smiling on a mountaintop—not forgetting what day it was, but remembering and rejoicing that yes, it was Father's Day; yes, we were sad; and yes, we were also having an absolute blast. I even captured a video of Brave saying with his sweet, tender voice, "It's Father's Day and we're doing something that our daddy used to love."

Choosing Redemption

There is a stark difference between restoration and redemption. We may never be able to restore all that was lost, but we can choose to redeem it. As you think about the calendar year, what days feel for you the way Father's Day feels for me? What holidays, celebrations, or anniversaries stir up feelings of dread, sadness, or anxiety? Maybe it's the birthday of a loved one who has passed away or the wedding anniversary of a marriage that ended in divorce. Maybe it's Christmas or Thanksgiving and life doesn't look the way you thought it would. Maybe it's Valentine's Day and you are once again flooded with feelings of loneliness.

Milestones and holidays never seem to end. We make it through one just in time for another. Early on in my journey as a widow, I was given some sage advice from a friend familiar with grief. She said, "If you don't decide how the day will go, the day will decide for you." And I've held onto those words ever since. On some significant days, such as Andrew's birthday, I make big plans to celebrate. Every year on May 19, my sons and I honor him with a bonfire at the beach. We bring all his favorite snacks and grab a bundle of firewood, some pizzas, and a few cozy blankets before heading down to the sand to watch the sunset. We swap our favorite Andrew stories, laughing about his love for candy, his curated collection of cozy robes and slippers, and how he enjoyed the freedom of walking around the house in his "birthday suit."

Yet on other significant days, such as the anniversary of his death, I find it very difficult to make a plan. I never know for certain how I am going to feel. Will I want to be alone or with family and friends? Will I want to visit the cemetery or sit at his favorite lifeguard tower at the beach? Will I feel overwhelmed with emotion as my body relives the trauma from that fateful day, or will I feel empty and numb? I've learned throughout the years that some of these significant days demand more flexible plans. Sometimes our grief needs the freedom to feel whatever it needs to feel without the constraint of a schedule. Yes, we can choose to redeem and reclaim the power of these difficult days, but it's perfectly okay not to be okay on other days. As we consider how to plan ahead, shift the narrative, and heal our harder days, may we remember to intentionally create space for grace. Feelings should never be forced. We can welcome *what is* with gentleness as we begin to dream up new possibilities of what a new narrative could be.

New Traditions

Perhaps another way to redeem the more difficult days is through establishing new traditions. When the future feels grim, new traditions can give us something to look forward to. During my first year as a widow, I started two new traditions with my three sons: a weekly tradition of Friday night movie night and a holiday tradition of Christmas in Colorado. Both of these traditions have released joy in a really special way. Every Friday night we order pizza, snuggle up in the living room with overflowing bowls of popcorn and candy, and enjoy a movie together. And every Christmas we hop on an airplane and fly to Colorado to spend a week visiting family and playing in the snow. While neither of these traditions eradicates our grief or our pain, they do weave new joy into the tapestry of our story. While it may feel like much of what made life beautiful before is gone, we have the opportunity to create a new kind of beautiful right here too.

It is not a betrayal of our loss to start something new. The truth is, seasons of change or loss require adjusting. As the saying goes, "We cannot direct the wind, but we can adjust our sails." Although present reality is irreversible, the past is still a sacred part of who we are because we carry our life experiences forward with us. No one can take away the love we have shared, the joy we have encountered, or the beautiful memories we have made. Those precious gifts are ours forever. When we shift our focus from all we've lost to all we have received, we can look toward the past with gratitude and step toward the future without being disabled by grief. Change is inevitable. Stepping toward healing means accepting that everything is fleeting. When we know nothing lasts forever, this knowledge should beckon us to appreciate the gifts right in front of us all the more.

To Make Whole

The word *healing* literally means to make something whole. As we welcome *what is*, and as we courageously begin to create something new, my hope is that one day our hearts will be made whole again. The Japanese art of kintsugi is such a striking example of what our hearts look like after healing from grief. Over four hundred years ago, the technique was developed to take broken pieces of pottery and repair them with gold to create an even stronger and more beautiful piece of art. The artist doesn't try to hide the flaws or imperfections; instead the goal is to embrace the shattered pieces as part of the sacred whole. The scars are an important part of the design. What a powerful metaphor for us to remember in our sorrow. The goal of healing isn't to hide our pain or conceal the broken parts of our story; instead it is to declare that our scars make us beautiful. Our scars make us unique, strong, resilient, tender, and tough.

You, my friend, are a beautiful work of art. No matter how old you are, no matter how many times your life has fallen apart, no matter how bleak your circumstance, you have the opportunity to pick up the pieces of your once shattered life and create something new. Establish a weekly tradition. Celebrate the significant days when you can. Book a trip to your favorite destination. Invite new joy to seep into the cracks and carry you through. No more excuses. No more clinging to *what was*, wishing your present wasn't your reality. You are here. Your story is significant. And a brand-new, beautiful narrative is being birthed within you.

The goal of healing
isn't to hide our pain or
conceal the broken parts
of our story; instead it
is to declare that our
scars make us beautiful.

Redemption is the heart of God. Scripture is full of hope-filled stories of real people who fought bravely and overcame significant challenges. Remember the story of Joseph? A man betrayed by his own brothers, sold into slavery, and forced onto a completely different course? He had every reason to be bitter, angry, and resentful toward God and his family, but he chose redemption instead. He partnered with God to create a brand-new, beautiful, and meaningful life. Through Joseph, God saved a whole nation from starvation. Joseph's story is so moving and powerful, it was even adapted as a musical on Broadway.

It makes me wonder: What redemption story does God have in store for me and for you? What's the new thing he wants to do right here in the midst of our rebuilding? Just like Joseph, we can't write a brand-new narrative on our own. Only when we partner with God in the process can we see how he truly works all things—the lovely, the horrific, the painful, and the beautiful—together for good. I love these powerful words from the apostle Paul:

Meanwhile, the moment we get tired in the waiting, God's Spirit is right alongside helping us along. If we don't know how or what to pray, it doesn't matter. He does our praying in and for us, making prayer out of our wordless sighs, our aching groans. He knows us far better than we know ourselves . . . That's why we can be so sure that every detail in our lives of love for God is worked into something good. (Rom. 8:26–28 MSG)

When we don't know how to face the painful days, and when we don't know what to say or even how to pray, we can trust that God is with us. We can surrender our own agenda in exchange for his redemption plan. Even in the most horrific or pain-filled circumstance, we can partner with his love to create a life that's meaningful, beautiful, and good.

CHAPTER 6

DOING THE WORK

> There are two extremes to avoid: being
> completely absorbed in your pain and being
> distracted by so many things that you stay
> far away from the wound you want to heal.
> —Henri Nouwen

Rebuilding beautiful isn't just an external journey of creating a picture-perfect life; it's an internal journey of embracing the messy parts of our story as part of the beautiful whole. This is where we show up to do important work of welcoming and working through our trauma. We can engage in the work of healing from wherever we are, but it's most common for this work to involve partnering with experts in the field of trauma and mental health.

I was a senior in high school when I had my first encounter with a mental health professional. Ongoing tension in our home had led our family to finally reach out for help. The first place we turned to was our church, which offered Christian counseling services. We arrived at our session to find five chairs forming a circle, one for the counselor and the other four for our family. The session did not go well. We each took a turn talking about the temperature of our home. Emotions heightened and morphed into anger, and we left in a flurry of tears. I remember feeling absolutely mortified. The church was an important part of my world growing up. It was my safe haven—a place where I felt loved, seen, valued, and connected. Our family drama didn't belong there; our issues were invading my otherwise happy space.

After that day at the church, things continued to unravel at home and hit a breaking point on Easter morning 2007. It was the day that changed everything for our family. A final argument, a final straw that broke the camel's back. The relationship between my parents was over, and like many children who experience a divorce I felt my heart was torn in two. I didn't want to take sides, but I felt like a side was being chosen for me. It was all too much to wrap my young mind around. The foundation of my world was crumbling, and I couldn't find solid ground anywhere. By the time I graduated high school, I started to count down the days until I could run away to college and leave it all behind.

But I didn't. When I finally made it to college, all my unprocessed emotional trauma came with me. I remember recounting the events of Easter with new friends on the dorm room floor as tears streamed down my face. I remember looking for someone to take me in for the summer break and holidays because I didn't feel like I had a home to return to. I remember feeling lost within myself as I searched for belonging.

It took years to finally move beyond that Easter day, and more than a decade to even have eyes to see the trauma from all of its many angles. My parents had carried unprocessed trauma from their adolescent years into their marriage, then tried their best to raise a family and create a beautiful life with the tools they had been given. But trauma, when left unprocessed, will travel through families until someone is brave enough to feel it. When we ignore our trauma or try to bury the hurt, we aren't solving the problem—only delaying the work that needs to be done and creating more dysfunction for years to come. As the author Richard Rohr wrote, "If we do not transform our pain, we will most assuredly transmit it."[1] Perhaps the greatest gift we can give ourselves, our kids, or even our grandkids is to finally be brave enough to face and embrace our pain. We have the power to let the cycle of generational trauma stop with us. We don't need to be bound by the chains of pain anymore. To step into healing is to step into the freedom that's been waiting for us all along.

Approaches to Healing Trauma

There is no one-size-fits-all approach when it comes to recovering from trauma. The joy of doing the work is discovering what works best for you! As I've explored my own trauma, I have engaged many means of healing.

1. Talk Therapy (Psychotherapy)

The first approach I experienced, and perhaps the most common approach many of us are familiar with, is talk-based therapy or psychotherapy. Before Andrew and I were married, we went through premarital counseling. While Andrew was battling depression, we attended marriage counseling. And after Andrew's suicide, I spent years unpacking my trauma in the safety of individual counseling. For two years individual counseling was part of my weekly routine: just one hour out of my week to show up and do the work. Even when I didn't want to go, I went. Even when I didn't feel like tapping into my pain, I opened up anyway.

The gift of scheduling therapy sessions in advance was knowing that when painful emotions erupted or unexpected events occurred, I would always have someone to talk to. There were even a few sessions when the timing was impeccable. For example, on the morning of a scheduled therapy session, I received a text from my mother-in-law that said: "Andrew's headstone was installed today." I had just enough time to visit the cemetery before counseling. After seeing my late husband's name, birth date, and death date etched in stone for the first time, I walked into therapy weeping. My therapist wept with me, sat with me, and listened without judgment as I processed every ugly emotion out loud.

Friends, talk therapy is a gift. Having a neutral space to be completely real and vulnerable is priceless. That inner dialogue you would never share with anyone? You can share it in therapy. Those questions you wouldn't dare ask out loud? You can ask them in therapy. And those fears you have been bottling up? You can release them in therapy. If you feel like you have no one to talk to, there is a therapist who would love to connect with you.

> Having a neutral space to be completely real and vulnerable is priceless.

Maybe you have a therapist, but you aren't getting what you need. Or maybe the chemistry simply isn't there. If so, you can always search for someone new. Finding the right therapist is sort of like dating; it may take many "dates" until you feel like you've found the right fit, and that's totally okay! There is no such thing as a perfect therapist, but if therapy isn't serving you the way it ought to, you don't have to stay stuck in the therapeutic relationship. When you've found the right therapist, you'll know!

2. Movement

Moving my body as a way to release stored trauma has also been a gift. When I first started exercising after my loss, I felt very disconnected from my body. As I lifted dumbbells in my garage, I knew my arms were moving, but I felt detached and numb. My therapist encouraged me to continue exercising and was hopeful that I would eventually feel embodied again, and I did. The beauty of exercise is that it works! Numerous studies have proven that daily exercise has positive effects on all areas of the body, including our minds. Exercise stimulates the brain and helps the nervous system restore balance by burning off adrenaline and releasing endorphins. Exercise also improves sleep, reduces stress, boosts self-esteem, and helps fight off feelings of depression and anxiety.[2]

For many of us in a season of transition, change, or loss, the thought of exercise can feel daunting, but it doesn't have to be. We can start small. Maybe a ten-minute walk around the neighborhood is enough for today. Maybe you'd like to try something new, like dusting off that unused paddleboard you've stored away, or enrolling in that hot yoga class your friends keep inviting you to. Maybe you'd want to purchase a stationary bike or check out a CrossFit class! For me, exercise is following along with a thirty-minute workout video from the comfort of my living room. Whatever you choose to do, know you are not only releasing powerful endorphins, but also allowing your stored-up trauma to move through you.

3. Spiritual Direction

Trauma affects the mind and the body, but it also affects the soul. As it's been said before: "You don't have a soul; you are a soul, and you have a body." The soul is the essence of our being, the part of us that never dies. So it makes sense that our souls would also be impacted by our suffering. If you hope to pursue inner healing at a soul level, a spiritual director can be greatly beneficial. Spiritual direction is not therapy; it is a practice found in many religious traditions that focuses on exploring faith and a relationship with God for healing. Through active listening, spiritual directors can guide us and redirect us back to God's presence in our lives and the world around us. As they listen to our stories, they can help us discover soul areas that are clinging to unforgiveness, disappointment, shame, guilt, or anger. Through healing prayer and intimate conversations, they can help us let go of the past, awaken to new possibilities and connections, or even uncover deeper meaning from the pain.[3]

4. Writing

During my first year of grief post-loss, I spent most of my days writing. All the words I wrote down for the purpose of my own healing became something I could offer others as captured in my first book, *Fear Gone Wild: A Story of Mental Illness, Suicide, and Hope Through Loss*. Writing my story down while the memories and the pain were still fresh was powerful. Most days I sat at my computer and typed through tears. Finding the words to describe my experience forced me to step toward my trauma in ways I otherwise wouldn't have. Sitting at my computer to type felt like therapy. The healing that poured out from my willingness to show up to do the work could never have come about otherwise.

Writing is beautiful because it knows no bounds. Your outlets are limitless, and your words don't have to become a book. The words could simply be a letter you write to yourself or to those who caused you pain. The words could become a poem, a song, or a prayer. The words could be as private as a diary or as public as a social media post. The bottom line is, writing is healing. Studies have proven that expressive writing greatly benefits

73

our emotional and physical health. The practice not only helps us process what we've been through, but it can also reduce stress, anxiety, and depression; boost the immune system; improve sleep; lower blood pressure; and improve overall well-being.[4]

Sacred Scars

These are just a few of the many paths of healing. Find what works best for you and commit yourself to showing up. At first it may feel like ripping the Band-Aids from your wounds, but the hope is that eventually those wounds will heal and form scars in their place. The pain may lessen over time, but the scars remain sacred reminders of just how far we've come.

I find it fascinating that even Jesus had scars. After his crucifixion and resurrection, he visited his disciples. To prove his identity, he showed them the scars on his hands and his side. And immediately they recognized him and rejoiced (John 20:20). Our scars, like Jesus' scars, aren't something to hide away; instead, we can be identified by them. Our scars not only tell the stories of how we've healed and overcome; they can also offer hope to others who may wonder if their own wounds will ever heal.

Friend, show up for the hard work of healing, and wear your scars proudly. You've earned them. You've fought hard for them. And through them, you have a powerful story to tell. Just as we are healed through Christ's wounds (1 Peter 2:24), our wounds can help others find healing too.

EXPLORE

(transitive verb): to investigate, study, or analyze; look into; to become familiar with[1]

Afew years ago, before the global pandemic, I had the opportunity to visit the beautiful country of Australia with some friends. We were planning to drink all the flat whites we could get our hands on, waste all our money on silly tourist traps in Sydney, and attend a special women's conference called Colour. It was hands down one of my favorite trips of all time. We visited the Sydney Opera House, walked the coast of Bondi Beach, and stayed out until the wee hours of the morning at an underground speakeasy. We had high tea in the afternoon, soaked up sessions at the conference, and even took a ferry ride around the harbor. But the absolute highlight of the trip was when we climbed the Sydney Harbour Bridge.

We had contemplated booking the bridge climb all week, then finally decided one night to book a climb for the following day. When we woke in the morning, it was pouring rain. I mean, absolutely pouring—the most rain Sydney had seen in months. We called to see if we could get a refund on the climb, but their policy clearly stated "rain or shine." So we braved the rain and showed up anyway! We slid into the obnoxious blue jumpsuits, zipped up our black raincoats, and began our climb up 1,332 stairs to the top. It was raining so hard we could barely see our feet, and every spectacular view of the city was completely washed away. When we neared the summit, my friend Tawnee and I—drenched from head to toe, mascara dripping down our cheeks, sneakers squeaking, and hair soaking wet—caught a serious case of the giggles. We were laughing so hard we had to stop and sit down on the stairs. The situation was just so far from what we had expected it to be, we had no choice but to throw our hands in the air and have a good laugh!

This is the mystery of exploration: when we show up to try something new and aren't able to control the elements or predict the outcome. The joy is in the journey. When we are brave enough to step foot out of our comfort zones, the results may surprise us! That's what we are going after in this next section. We've embraced our pain and shown up for the hard work of healing—so now we get to have some fun! Through the next three chapters, we will explore ways to encounter love after loss, the impact of suffering on our faith, and the beauty of showing up to try something new in the midst of rebuilding our lives.

CHAPTER 7

WORTHY OF LOVE

> You are imperfect, you are wired for
> struggle, but you are worthy of love and
> belonging.
>
> —BRENÉ BROWN

Before you read another word, I just need you to know you are
worthy of love. Your circumstances aren't too much. Your
problems aren't too big. Your grief is not a burden. Your children
are not baggage. You—all of you, everything you bring to the
table—are worthy of the beautiful gift of love.

If you haven't lost a spouse or aren't in the dating pool right
now, I still believe there is something for you in this chapter.

Maybe you are walking alongside a loved one who has encountered a season of singleness. Or maybe you, too, even in your relationship or marriage, feel utterly alone. The truth is, after a traumatic experience, many of us are flooded with intrusive thoughts of doubt, criticism, and frustration. Pain changes us, and it changes our relationships. It changes how we interact with the world around us. It changes how we welcome and embrace love. The person I am today—the life experience I have to offer and the love I have to share—is radically different from the twenty-one-year-old who first said "I do" to Andrew.

As I've approached dating again, I've done so with both caution and trepidation. It's a strange experience going from a well-worn kind of love to square one. It's an even stranger reality to be returning in your thirties to square one with three children. I've often wondered if there's even room for new love. My children, my work, my hobbies, my dreams, and my ambitions all take up plenty of space. *When would I even have time to date? How can I create space for someone new when I feel like my world is already fuller than full?*

These are questions I continue to ask myself. As I write these words to you, I am dating but still very much single. The driving force of my curiosity about dating again is the thought of my future self. I know my life won't always look the way it does today. One day my three boys will grow up, leave home, and pave their own way in the world. And I will be left all alone. That picture of a potentially lonely future is enough for me to bravely say yes to a date today. And I have.

My first date as a widow just happened to be with a widower.

He "slid into my DMs" on social media, and after several weeks of lengthy phone conversations, we decided to meet. I had an upcoming trip for a conference near his hometown, so it worked out perfectly. He picked me up from my hotel, and we headed toward the water—both of us a little awkward and uncomfortable, both of us knowing what it's like to lose it all, and both of us trying to be brave enough to find it again. We filled an ice chest with snacks and drinks, climbed into a little boat made for two, and slowly paddled our way to a small island in the middle of a lake. We poured margaritas into red Solo cups and toasted to the strangeness, beauty, brokenness, and mystery of things. Our hearts cracked, yet they still beat with hope over the possibility of new love. It was so picture-perfect and magical, I felt like a contestant on an episode of *The Bachelor*.

On our way back to the hotel to change for dinner, we saw some kids jumping off a bridge into the water below. My date looked at me with a cheeky smile, pulled to the side of the road, and ran over to join them. He begged me to jump with him—to let go, to live in the moment—but I shook my head no. In so many ways, I wasn't ready to jump all the way in. He threw his head back and laughed because he knew I was already trying so hard to be brave.

We freshened up and headed to a local spot on the water for dinner. It was an old, run-down restaurant, the kind that serves up greasy meals on parchment paper in red plastic baskets. We walked through the doors and discovered a cover band playing live country music, creating the dreamy kind of ambience you could only hope for on a first date. We decided to enjoy our dinner outside on a quaint empty dock. As the sun painted the sky with hues of pink, purple, and blue, we sat, just the two of us, drinking cold beers and working our way through the delicious, greasy food. It was a sacred, healing moment. Even if we never saw each other again, showing up scared and brave together was something special we could hold onto. He drove me back to my hotel, beat me in a game of chess in the lobby, and kissed me goodbye. And that was that: a first date and a last. We both headed back to our broken realities and haven't seen each other since.

The Gift of Time

This is dating on the other side of loss. This is what it looks like to hold it all loosely, knowing great love can't be forced or rushed. If I've learned anything, it's that time is my friend on the journey to finding love again after losing it.

> Time is my friend on the journey to finding love again after losing it.

Time is a gift that offers room for us to grieve and heal before we give our hearts away. Time gives us space to grow with our pain so we can have eyes to see both the wreckage and the route forward toward beauty. At the start of a new course—post-loss, post-divorce, or post-breakup—we are so close to our pain that it's hard to even grasp the totality of it. How could we possibly be ready to date again when we haven't fully processed all that we have lost? Taking the time to step toward healing before stepping toward the next date will not only benefit us in the present moment; it will also benefit us in the future.

There are many paths for rebuilding a beautiful life, especially for those who've loved and lost but desire to find love again. And one great mystery of love is that it doesn't respect our timelines. Some find it quickly, and more than once, while others spend an entire lifetime searching for it. Grieving a lost relationship is painful and unpleasant, and it may be tempting to rush into falling in love again, fixing what was broken, or filling an empty void. But time is one of the greatest graces we can give ourselves in grief—space to mourn all that was lost, to take inventory of our fragile emotions, and to slowly wrap our minds around our hopes and desires for the next relationship. As it's been said, "You can't rush something you want to last forever."

Perhaps you are reading this from the perspective of a current marriage or relationship. Maybe another major life change—a big move, a career shift, a retirement, or even a tragic loss—has changed the dynamics of your relationship. Time is your friend too. Take time to work on yourself so you can pour out your love from a place that is healed and secure. And take time to get to know your spouse again. Who are they on the other side of this experience? How has the loss changed them? How can you come alongside them as they step into a new version of themselves? The truth is, you didn't just marry the person you said "I do" to on your wedding day; you also married all the versions of that person you have yet to meet. Some versions are more pleasant than the others (which is where the "for better or for worse" part comes in).

I truly believe that a season of rebuilding doesn't have to destroy a relationship. Just as you built a life together in the beginning, you can build a new life together now. It will, however, take effort to get to know each other again in this season. If you feel rejected, if you feel like a burden, or even if you feel unworthy of love in your current relationship, seek help. Seek wise counsel. Be brave enough to be honest with your spouse. And remember that even in a worn-in relationship, you are still worthy of great love.

Vulnerability and Fear

After that magical first date, I decided to say yes to another date—this time with a divorcé who kindly offered to fly into town just to take me out to dinner. I'm a sucker for a romantic gesture, so it was an easy yes. I daydreamed about the date with friends, wondering what it would be like to meet him in person for the first time. When the day came, I was full of fluttering emotions and nervous butterflies. I hopped in my car to drive down the coast to meet him for dinner. On my drive, I had one of those indescribable moments. The sun was setting on the sea, and I listend to a familiar song about starting over. As I sped down the highway, staring out at the vast open ocean, all I could think about was my future self and how proud she would be of me—stepping out into new possibilities, opening my broken but hopeful heart to new love.

This date was just as dreamy as the last. We ate our way through downtown San Diego, including drinks at a bar, dinner at a fancy restaurant, and dessert at a small French café. Conversation flowed freely and easily between two creative spirits with so much in common. We both loved writing, reading, and even running. Yet, at the end of our date as we said our goodbyes, I drove home knowing that first date would also be our last. He was everything wonderful, but I still wasn't ready for love.

One hard part of exploring romantic relationships after losing the love of your life is that you never stop loving the person you lost. When I told this kind man on the phone that I couldn't go on another date, I literally said to him, "If there was a lineup of guys and Andrew was standing in the line, I would pick him every single time." How could I give my heart away to someone when it's still held by a man who isn't even here? That's another wild thing about love: it's really hard to let it go.

So here I sit today, pouring my heart into these words. I'm three years a widow, with two measly dates under my belt and a whole future in front of me. Will I get married again one day? I hope so. Will I meet him soon? Maybe. Will I find happiness either way? Absolutely. If I've learned anything over the last three years, it's that our happiness isn't held in anyone's hands but our own. We are the keepers of our own joy. A man will never make me whole. My hope is that I will already be well on the road to healing and wholeness before I fall in love again. I'm not looking for anybody to complete me—just someone to run alongside me as I run alongside them too.

Don't Settle for Less

We don't have to settle for less. Whether you are married, in a relationship, or single again, you are deserving of deep love. You deserve kindness and respect. Just because life has thrown some curveballs your way doesn't mean you have to lower your standards. Take time to heal. Set the bar high. Believe great love is waiting in the wings for you.

> Take time to heal. Set the bar high. Believe great love is waiting in the wings for you.

And for those of us in a season of singleness, it's okay to tread lightly. We don't have to search for another relationship from a place of desperation. Before we step toward the next date, we can stop to ask ourselves why. *Am I trying to avoid feelings like hurt, anger, sadness, or loneliness? Or am I moving from a place of healing?* Dating comes with its own set of challenges and emotions. If we aren't emotionally healthy, we might not be ready to embrace the uncertainty and vulnerability that dating will require. Then again, perhaps we will never know the answers to these questions unless we try. Was I ready for either of those dates I went on? I'm not sure. But what I do know is that I have learned new things about myself and the kind of love I'm looking for in the process, and I refuse to settle for less.

Made to Love and Be Loved

The truth is, we were made to love and be loved. Love is woven into the world around us. Love is the main theme in nearly every story line on TV. Love is at the heart of the books we read, the songs we sing, and the affection we pour over others. Love is in the tears we cry when someone dies and even the happy tears that fall when we rejoice. So why wouldn't we crave it in our relationships and search for it again after we've lost it? It's just so wonderful, so mysterious, so utterly indescribable. Love is what heaven must be like: that euphoric feeling of being deeply seen, known, and cared for. We crave it from the minute we are born. We are always reaching out for love.

As we reach out for the beautiful gift of love, may we remember it is already reaching out for us too. Absolutely nothing can get in the way of this powerful gift. No matter how many lies we believe about ourselves or our circumstances, no matter how high we build the walls around our fragile hearts, and no matter how isolated, lonely, or desperate we may feel, love is always there. In Paul's powerful letter to the Roman church, he wrote about the power of God's love: "I'm absolutely convinced that nothing— nothing living or dead, angelic or demonic, today or tomorrow, high or low, thinkable or unthinkable—absolutely *nothing* can get between us and God's love" (Rom. 8:39 MSG).

As you heal your broken heart and fight to rebuild a beautiful life, may you welcome and embrace the precious gift of love that surrounds you. Even if you were never to experience the joy of romantic love again, it wouldn't mean you are loved any less. You are deeply loved, right where you are, just as you are. Single or married, widowed or divorced, lonely or surrounded by community—love is holding you close the whole way through.

CHAPTER 8

THE CRISIS OF FAITH

The secret is Christ in me, not me in a
different set of circumstances.

—Elisabeth Elliot

I don't know a life without faith. It's been part of my reality since
the beginning. In my home growing up, we were a family that
prayed around the dinner table every night and dressed in our
best clothes for church every Sunday. My faith has been the one
constant I can count on and return to relentlessly. During the
times when the world around me felt unsafe and uncertain, my
faith has seen me through. To hope that there is an Author of
my story who has gone before me, who has already written the

next line, and who wants the absolute best for me—why wouldn't I want to believe in a love like that? Who wouldn't want to be known, to be seen, and to be cared for with such tender intimacy?

Faith is about mystery—having confidence, hope, and assurance in the things we cannot fully see. There has always been more than meets the eye—always something deeper happening beneath the surface of our experiences. There will always be things we can never understand. Even science has its limitations. Mystery is embedded everywhere, in everything. I see it in the wonder of my children's eyes, in the beauty of the cotton candy sunset sky, and in the tears that flow at the graveside. We were never meant to have all the answers. We've been surrendering to the divine mystery all along.

Faith Without Formulas

I've always thought that prayer is simply talking to God: a time to thank him for all he's done and to ask for the things that have yet to come. This simplistic transactional prayer works for a while, when life is good and problems are minimal. Life is good when we "name it and claim it" or "have enough faith to believe it," or when all the things we pray for and ask for come to pass. But what happens when something goes wrong with the transaction? You prayed passionately for a loved one to be cured from cancer, but she wasn't. You worked hard, prayed, and deeply believed you would receive the promotion at work, but it was given to someone else. You begged God to stop the chaos swirling in your depressed loved one's mind, but then he died by suicide. You have tried for years to get pregnant, but every attempt has failed. If you believe in a transactional God, then any undesired outcomes will lead you to question your own efforts. You may wonder: *Did I pray hard enough? Do I have enough faith? Did I do something wrong? Do I have a sin issue? Why didn't God hear me? Why didn't he answer my prayer the way I asked him to?*

All these questions can lead to guilt and shame. We may start to believe we aren't good enough, our faith isn't strong enough, we didn't pray hard enough, or we are missing the mark in some way. We may even strive harder to do better—believing that if we do, we can somehow earn an easy life. But we were never promised an easy life. The stories we read in Scripture aren't pretty and polished. They are messy—full of drama, suffering, beauty, misery, and mystery intertwined. Faith isn't a mathematical problem to be solved. We may never find the answers we are searching for, and we may never understand why God allowed our suffering to be filtered through his hands. No matter how much beauty and redemption we find on the other side of loss, the pain may always sting.

When the formula for our faith doesn't work anymore, we are forced to find another way. We can walk away from God completely, believing he failed us in our hour of need. We can stew in shame and guilt believing it wasn't God who failed us but our own failing efforts. Or we can choose to open our eyes to a new way of approaching the faith journey: a way that allows our suffering to lead us closer to a deeper truth; a way that challenges us to sees things differently, expands our faith, and makes room for our pain.

My encounter with great suffering has led to a new way of seeing everything. When Andrew was battling depression, I begged God for a breakthrough and truly believed God would heal him. I believed God would lead us to the right doctors, to the right medication, or to supernatural intervention. We had our faith, we had our love, and we had a beautiful future ahead of us; this was just a detour, and we would be back on track in no time. But as I prayed for months, God felt silent. I remember saying out loud, *"Where are you, God? Why aren't you fixing this? Why are you allowing this to happen?"*

And then Andrew died. The depression wasn't a detour after all; it led to our complete derailment. So again I asked, *"Where are you, God?"* And the answer I've found here on the other side of loss is that God is everywhere. Loss has opened my eyes to the divine mystery all around me. In the tiny flower that has fought to find its way through the cracks in the pavement. In the sparkle of the sunlight that dances and shimmers on the sea. In the giggles that echo through the halls after I've told my boys it's time to go to sleep. In the colors of a rainbow after a gray and stormy day. It's as if God has been whispering all along: "Look for the rainbow, and remember My promise" (Gen. 9:17 The Voice).

When I think about rainbows and the mystery of God all around me, a special photo will always come to my mind. It was captured at the end of a rainy day in September in California. One Friday (Andrew's one day off each week), we enjoyed a lazy day of extra snuggles, hot cocoa, and a movie marathon as a family. When the rain finally stopped, we headed into the backyard to play, and on display in the sky over our home was a beautiful rainbow. I grabbed my phone to take a picture, and as I did, Andrew began tossing our son Brave into the sky, catching him as he giggled from being lobbed up so high. I snapped a few photos and was surprised to see the beauty of what I captured. From the angle of my camera, Brave seemed to be flying. Dressed only in a diaper, his sweet little body soared through the air—well above the ten-foot wall in our backyard, arms stretched out wide and positioned perfectly under the arch of the rainbow. Andrew stood right below him with a sweet smirk on his face, ready to catch our baby as he dropped back to the earth.

A few years later, in the midst of the long days of distance learning brought on by COVID-19, this photo resurfaced. As we sat around our white wooden table, I read the first task of the day: a writing prompt. It began: "One day I saw a rainbow . . ." As the sound of rain echoed through old single-pane windows, we sat together and wrote about rainbows. From the end of his pen, my seven-year-old, Smith, poured his little heart into the words: "One day I saw a rainbow in my backyard. My dad threw my brother Brave in the sky. My mama took a picture."

In that moment, all I could think was, *I'm so glad Mama took a picture.* With three busy boys surrounding me, I pulled out my phone and scrolled back a few years to find the old photo we loved. We all smiled big at our boy Brave, flying high through the air as a rainbow arched through the clouds.

As we move through the storms that will inevitably come, our job isn't to try to control the weather; instead we are to

Yes, there will be rain, but there will be rainbows too.

"trace the rainbow through the rain."[1] We can hold onto the hope of peace in the midst of our deepest uncertainties. And we can let go of our relentless pursuit of answers to every unanswerable question as we remember there is beauty to be found even in the things we will never understand. Yes, there will be rain, but there will be rainbows too.

Expanding Our Approach

Many of us on this journey of rebuilding beautiful are recovering from the impact of great suffering. We are on the other side of an encounter with one of the greatest mysteries of life: pain. We thought we had it all figured out, and we thought we knew exactly how things would pan out—but here we are in a completely different reality. When our hearts were ripped open, so were our eyes. We will never be the same or see the same. Retreating to the past isn't an option; forward is the only way to go. To work toward the beauty of *what could be*, we must welcome *what is* and walk through it courageously.

As we consider how to engage, expand, or deepen our relationship with God here in this new life, maybe it's time to approach faith differently. In my journey of rebuilding beautiful, practices of contemplation, centering prayer, and meditation on Scripture have all been greatly healing in my approach to faith.

1. The Gift of Contemplation

I love this definition of contemplation: "the practice of being fully present—in heart, mind, and body—to *what is* in a way that allows you to creatively respond and work toward *what could be*."[2] To be "fully present" means rewiring our often cluttered and distracted minds to focus on what is right in front of us. Whether it be a conversation with a friend, a mundane moment with our children, standing at the sink washing dishes, folding a pile of laundry, sitting in our cubicle at work, or staring out at an open horizon, being present is about honoring God and having an awareness of him in every moment. When we have eyes to see God in everything, our relationship with him becomes boundless—not confined to a set time of the day and not about getting something in return. Instead, we can experience a completely different way of approaching faith and life. We can now encounter the divine everywhere, in everything, all the time. This is how we make our lives a prayer or "pray without ceasing" (1 Thess. 5:17 ESV). Time with God becomes less about forced connection and more about a conscious awareness of his presence and active involvement in our life. It's not about changing the reality that's in front of us; it's about having new eyes to see our reality differently. Perhaps the secret to encountering God in the midst of our suffering is to recognize that he's already there with us.

2. Centering Prayer

Another daily practice that can help us awaken to God's presence is centering prayer. Centering prayer is simply sitting in silence, open to God's love and our love for God. It's a practice of realigning a cluttered mind. The goal of centering prayer is to dismantle our ego's desire for control so we can surrender to the flow of God's love moving within, through, and around. To practice centering prayer, we can choose a word—usually one or two syllables is best—such as *God, love, peace, grace, Jesus, trust,* or *faith.* Then we take as little or as much time as we need to sit quietly with it. When the mind starts to wander—and it will—gently try to return to the chosen word and rest calmly in God's presence.

When we consistently practice centering prayer, we are so deeply connected to God's presence and love that it changes the way we respond to everyday moments. The goal is for centering prayer to carry beyond prayer time and into our lives in this way. Where we would have formerly been inclined to react out of emptiness, exhaustion, or frustration, we can now gently respond with a heart of love. As a mom of three very active young boys, this practice has helped me calm my own inner storm so I can foster a peaceful environment in my home.

3. Meditating on Scripture

Another way to unleash God's supernatural peace and healing is through Scripture. I have my own little routine when it comes to carving out time to pray and read Scripture. I first read a daily devotional (*Streams in the Desert* by Lettie Cowman and *You Are the Beloved* by Henri Nouwen are two of my favorite devotionals), followed by one chapter from Scripture. Then I read a chapter or two in an encouraging faith-based book and write down any thoughts, prayers, and reflections in my journal. When I spend time meditating on Scripture at the start of my day, something inside of me shifts. The practice reminds me that I'm not alone and never far from God's supernatural love and peace. It also helps me to focus on the things I can't usually see, and to avoid getting too wrapped up in the frustrations and interruptions I will surely encounter throughout the day. It's a regular reminder to let go and return to the safety of God's love and truth as a compass for my daily life.

Invitations Everywhere

Earlier this week I was running around our house getting everything ready for our little family to be out of town for a few days. There was laundry to be folded, dishes to be washed and put away, floors to be mopped, toilets to be scrubbed, and even dinner to be made. All this hustle paused, though, when my son Smith and I noticed a butterfly sitting on the stucco wall of our garage. Butterflies have had a special place in our hearts since Andrew died: a reminder of our own transformation yet to come and the transformation happening in real time since Andrew's been gone. We crouched down really close and noticed the butterfly wasn't moving; it was just sitting there on the stucco—alive but very still, maybe even close to death. I urged Smith to hold it in his hands, to take in all its beautiful colors. Butterflies usually fly right by, so this was a sacred invitation to hold all its beauty in the palm of his hand.

So, Smith picked it up and carried it into the house to show his brothers. We all leaned in close and admired the butterfly. We could have missed the moment completely, but we didn't. We saw the moment exactly as it was: a gift, a special chance to soak in the beauty of life. Friend, that's what it's all about. To rebuild beautiful, to draw near to the presence of God in the midst of our pain, we simply have to open our eyes long enough to behold the sacredness of each moment. We are alive. We have breath in our lungs. We have love to give. What a journey. What a joy it is to be right here in this moment together. What a gift.

CHAPTER 9

I'M SO PROUD OF YOU FOR TRYING

You never fail until you stop trying.
—UNKNOWN

I never knew what I was capable of until I tried. For years I believed the lies of my own limitations. Phrases like "I could never do that" lived comfortably in my mind. I've never been the naturally confident type. As a child I was labeled "shy," and I carried that label with me for a long time because it felt safe to hide behind. It takes a wild amount of courage to finally decide to live outside the limitations others have set for us or we've set for ourselves. To believe we are capable of so much more than we think can often feel like some far-off dream. But what if it's not? What if the only thing standing between us and our realized dreams is our willingness to try?

This book is a product of my own willingness to try. There were so many times on this journey of writing these words when I wanted to throw in the towel; when I didn't know if I could find fifty thousand words to write; when I didn't know if I had much to say at all. But I chose to try—to put into words what it's been like to rebuild my own life. I hope it will inspire others to rebuild their own versions of beautiful too. *Maybe if I go first,* I thought, *others might be willing to do the same.*

One of the places I often worked on this book was at the skate park. My three sons are obsessed with the skate park. It's our home away from home. It is honestly a marvel to see all they can do with four small wheels and a wooden board. The names of the tricks alone are complicated—ollie, nollie, boneless, nose-grind, kickflip, 360, backside air, boardslide, 50/50, shuvit—and the list goes on and on. I sit on the sidelines and watch them fly through the air. I cringe as their little bodies take hard falls, but I am completely captivated by their resilience and willingness to get up and try the trick again until they've mastered it. Through watching them skate, I've learned that the key to becoming a successful skater is simply being willing to try. You have to show up fearlessly, or you will fall. You have to commit fully, or you won't land the trick. It's an all-or-nothing kind of sport. You show up knowing that hard falls are coming—but the falls are what make the sport so challenging and fun. Your battle wounds are part of your victory.

Then a few months ago, I got tired of watching my boys from the sidelines and decided to give skateboarding a try. I know the day is quickly coming when my boys will be "too cool" to skate around the skate park with their mom. I am well-aware that during these innocent years, I need to soak up every opportunity to join them in the fun. So we went to our local skate shop, and the boys helped me pick out a board, a helmet, and all the protective gear we could find. Then we drove to our favorite local skate park. I knew just by the smirks on the faces of the other boys at the park that I looked ridiculous—bright white helmet, elbow pads, kneepads, and wrist guards securely fastened. I was ready to take on the smallest ramp I could find in the park. Both excited and terrified! My son Smith stood beside me offering some pointers. "Bend your knees, lean forward, spread your feet farther apart." And then, "You've got this, Mom! Go!" And I went.

> Your battle wounds are part of your victory.

The second I rolled down that tiny ramp, the board flew out from under my feet, and I fell flat on my back. I gathered up my pride, we had a good laugh, and then I got up to try again—and again and again. By the fifth or sixth try, I started to catch on: arms stretched out wide for balance, feet firmly planted on the board, knees bent, and fully committed to "sending it," as the skaters say. And I did! When I finally rolled down that tiny ramp without falling, Smith came running over, jumping up and down, with a smile stretched across his face. He leaned in to give me a big, proud hug. "Mom, you did it!" he said. "Now let's try that bigger one over there." My victory was short-lived, as it was soon followed by a hard fall down a ramp my boys nicknamed "the waterfall." I left the skatepark that day with a giant throbbing scrape on my arm, a big bruise on my hip, and a body sore from head to toe, but I was totally proud of myself for trying. Turns out skateboarding is a lot harder than it looks. I have so much to learn, but I am having so much fun learning alongside my sweet sons!

Choose Your Own Adventure

My adventure in skateboarding is not much different from my adventure in rebuilding my life. There have been so many moments when I, on the verge of trying something new, have stopped to ask myself, *Am I making a huge mistake? How will this impact my boys? Can I handle this? Am I making the right decision?* That last question is the one I've sat with the most. I think sometimes we put so much pressure on making the "right" decision that we never make a decision at all. What if there aren't any "right" decisions? What if life is simply about choosing our own adventure?

When I was a kid, the "choose your own adventure" books were popular. If you were born in the eighties or nineties, then you know exactly what I'm talking about. They were these fun interactive books where the reader got to make choices that determined the outcome of the plot. These books were so enjoyable because, in a way, the reader had the opportunity to become the author. Although the words were already written, it felt exciting to decide how the story would unfold. And if we didn't like the outcome of our decisions, we could go back and pick a different plot.

Much like these children's books, the journey of rebuilding a beautiful life might take a few tries to get right. We may make a big move to a new city and decide we want to move back home. We may pursue a new career and later decide we want to do something else. We may pick up a new hobby—like skateboarding!—but decide we don't like it after all. The beauty of life is that we have free will. We are the authors of our own stories. We have important roles to play in the outcome of the plot. We get to choose our own adventures. We get to try new things. We get to make mistakes. We get to change our minds.

About two years into my journey as a widow and single mom, I decided to go back to school to pursue a master's degree in psychology. It felt like the next right thing to do as I was already speaking and writing on the topic of mental health and suicide. I thought to myself, *If I am going to continue to engage the topic, why not become an expert?* So I applied to my alma mater, Vanguard University, went through the entire application and interview process, and was accepted! I was thrilled and so proud of myself for trying something new. I enrolled in classes, purchased the required textbooks, and began my journey of grad school. It was the fall of 2020, so my courses were virtual. I spent three nights a week in my home office on Zoom with twenty other students. The classes lasted for three hours, with a fifteen-minute break somewhere in the middle—the perfect amount of time to put my kids to sleep. Being a single parent is struggling to do it all well.

About six weeks into my adventure as a grad student, I realized it wasn't the right fit. The topics we discussed in class were hitting too close to home. I would often find myself drifting off and reliving my trauma as the professor was teaching. I couldn't focus on the content being taught because my experiences with it made it all too painful. So I made the decision to withdraw, and I am so glad I did. It would have been really easy to justify a decision to stay as "the right thing to do," but it wasn't the right thing for me and my healing. The classes were only causing me more pain.

Once I made the move to withdraw, I felt instant relief. It wasn't a waste of time or money because it was something I truly needed to try. If I hadn't, I may have spent a lot of time wondering, *What if I did?* That's another thing I'm learning here on the journey of rebuilding beautiful. We have to be willing to try new things, but we also have to be willing to step away when it's not the right thing.

Power Tools

Another fun adventure I've been having has been learning how to use power tools. In my life with Andrew, he always took care of things around the house. He hated when I attempted to hang decorations on the walls and would always find a roundabout way to tell me, "It's too high" or "It's crooked" or "It's too low." Also: "Are you sure you want that there?" and "Maybe you should wait for me to help next time." Over the years I eventually stopped trying. It wasn't worth the exhausting back and forth, and it usually turned out better when Andrew did it anyway. But since he's been gone, I've decided to try again. It started with wallpapering my bedroom, and since then, I've gotten into some serious home DIY. I now own a nail gun, a compressor, a table saw, a tile saw, and even a jigsaw. I installed board-and-batten down the hallway, vertical shiplap in all the bedrooms, and even gutted and renovated a bathroom. I've learned how to replace light fixtures and how to run a lawn mower. I even dug trenches and installed a brand-new sprinkler system in the front yard with the help of some neighbors and friends. If something breaks around the house now, I try to fix it on my own before reaching for the phone to call a professional. It's been incredibly empowering to stand in my home and see all the things I've made. I often throw my hands in the air and just laugh at how strange and surprising my life is. How shocked that girl who stopped trying would be to see what she was capable of all along. Are the home remodels perfect? No, not even close. If Andrew walked in, would he give me a few pointers? For sure! But it's a work in progress, it's cozy, and it's mine. And I'm just really glad I didn't let all those years of doubt scare me away from trying again.

Start Small

Maybe skateboarding, enrolling in grad school, or even learning how to use power tools sounds a little too ambitious. Trying something new doesn't have to take you all the way out of your comfort zone on the first attempt. Perhaps it starts with a little curiosity. If you want to try writing a book, maybe start with writing a blog. If you want to try becoming a fitness instructor, maybe start with a few classes. If you want to try pursuing a new career, maybe grab coffee with someone who is already doing it and ask a million questions. If you don't know where to start, start small. No one learns how to remodel a home, write a best-selling book, or kickflip a skateboard overnight. It takes time to develop the skills we need to be successful at the challenge we want to try. We just can't let the size of the dream scare us away.

When I was explaining to my dad all the renovations I wanted to make to our home, he looked me in the eyes and asked, "Hey, Kayla, do you know how to eat an elephant?" With a puzzled look on my face, I said, "No, how?"

He laughed a little, smiled, and said, "One bite at a time." I later Googled the phrase, and as it turns out, those are famous words from the highly respected bishop Desmond Tutu. Big tasks that may seem daunting, overwhelming, or even impossible can be accomplished by tackling them a little at a time. Maybe your life or your circumstance looks a bit like an elephant. The damage is so big, the mess is so messy, or the goal just seems way too far out of reach. But many successful people would confess that they didn't become successful overnight. They just showed up one day willing to try—then the next day and the next day—until one day they found themselves standing in a realized dream. No one eats an elephant in one bite; it's impossible. But because we have limitless potential waiting

The only thing standing between us and our beautiful dreams is our willingness to chase them and try!

to be tapped into, we can all start somewhere. The only thing standing between us and our beautiful dreams is our willingness to chase them and try!

Friend, you might take some hard falls, put a couple of holes in the wall, or even try something new and decide it's not for you. But just know this: You are capable—so much more capable than you think. Sometimes you just have to be brave enough to show up and try! I am so proud of you for trying. Know that I am right there with you, trying my best to show up too!

DREAM

(transitive verb): to consider as a possibility[1]

In my new life I've had many sleepless nights. During the first years of grief, many of those sleepless nights were spent reminiscing on *what was*. I could close my eyes and, like an old home movie, the reel of my former life would play in bright colors in my mind. *What was* was beautiful. On those nights, I would often pull out my phone and scroll for hours through my late husband's Instagram feed—our life in little boxes, captured and captioned by him, frozen in time, a precious gift.

One night as I lay there scrolling, an old black-and-white photo caught my eye. It was of a day I remember so well. I was eight months pregnant with our third boy, and we were in the process of building the home of our dreams. Though it was still under construction, we were captivated by the process—full of anticipation and excitement for *what could be*. In so many ways, that one black-and-white picture captured my current life as well: a life very much under construction. And that is what this section of the book is all about. As we hold *what was* in one hand and slowly grasp *what is* in the other, every single day is a brave step forward into *what could be*. The deeply painful journey of rebuilding a beautiful life is also hope-filled. In the next few chapters, we will explore what it looks like to dream beyond the destruction. We will examine how to take action on our dreams. And we will discover how to push through the many fears, roadblocks, and even people that may get in the way of us living out our beautiful dreams.

CHAPTER 10

HAPPY BEAUTIFUL LIFE

Create the highest, grandest vision possible
for your life because you become what you
believe.

—Oprah Winfrey

It was June 2019, and my boys and I were on an amazing adventure in Israel. After touring many historical sites throughout the country, we ended our trip with a few days in the city of Jerusalem. During our time in the city, we visited the famous Western Wall. This ancient limestone wall was a sight to take in all on its own. Standing over sixty feet tall, the Western Wall has been a mecca of religious pilgrimage and controversy for centuries. It is the only remaining structure of the Temple Mount, which was destroyed by the Romans in AD 70. I couldn't help but stand back in pure awe and reverence of the wall. The people there were shouting, reciting scripture, crying, and praying. On the wall itself, thousands of folded papers had been tucked into the crevices of the stone. Each paper represented a person and their hopes, dreams, wishes, and prayers.

This was a powerful and memorable moment, an opportunity for us to leave our own little mark on the ancient Wailing Wall. While my two youngest sons were cooling off in the shade with our friends from the tour, my oldest son, Smith, and I took some time to write a few notes. I told Smith he could write down whatever he wanted to leave at the wall. He grabbed a pencil and wrote three big words—"God's Got This"—three words that have been a mantra for our family for more than a decade. No matter what we go through in this life, we know we serve a God who is sovereign and in control. And on my paper, I wrote, "Happy Beautiful Life": the cry of my heart for my little family, for our life here on the other side of loss. Then we tucked the papers into the wall and continued on with our tour of Jerusalem.

But I've held onto that moment ever since. Those words continue to echo in my heart and in my mind. I want that happy beautiful life, not only for myself, but for my boys too. I want it here and now in this moment, and I want it for our future. All my audacious dreams can really be summed up in those three powerful words. But how do I get there? How do I move toward a life that's beautiful again? I truly believe the pathway is paved through daring to dream beyond the destruction. We have to close our eyes and imagine a beautiful future and then be willing to work hard to get there. I've heard it said before that an "imagined future transforms the present," but to get there, we might need a little vision.

New Vision

I'll never forget something one of my friends said to me during my first year of grief. First she asked: "What is your vision for the next five, ten, or fifteen years? What hopes and dreams do you have for your life?" And then came the kicker. She said, "Without vision, hope perishes." To hold onto hope of a beautiful future, we are going to need some vision.

If I asked you to close your eyes and picture yourself five years down the road, where would you be? Maybe you imagine holding a book that you wrote. Maybe you are holding a newborn baby in your arms. Maybe you are sitting in a big fancy office. Maybe you are running your first marathon. Maybe you are holding the keys to a new home. And then you open your eyes, but it's just a dream. It hasn't happened yet—so how do you get there? We can have a beautiful vision for the future, but without action and without tapping into resources we have available to us, our vision will never become reality. To arrive where we want to be, we have to push through our present reality. And to push through our present reality, we will need a little strategy. Even the most successful people had to start somewhere. You may not know where to start when it comes to accomplishing your dreams, but I bet with a little digging you will find plenty of resources within reach.

A few years ago my big beautiful dream was to write my first book, so I took some action steps. First, I gathered the resources I already had by reaching out to other authors in the publishing world. I asked them questions about the process, and they connected me with a book agent. My amazing book agent, Whitney, then directed me to first write a book proposal—basically an outline of what the book would be about—along with a few writing samples. When the book proposal was finished, Whitney sent it to several publishing houses. After a few publishers expressed interest, I went through a series of phone calls and interviews to pitch my book idea. Then I was thrilled to receive my first ever book deal. I signed the papers, committed to a manuscript due date, and then sat down to do the work. A few years later I stood in a realized dream, holding the very first printed copy of my book.

My dear friend Amy has a big beautiful dream of starting her own bourbon company. When she closes her eyes, she imagines herself standing on Wall Street ringing the bell that signals her company is open for trading. She imagines having enough money to buy homes for all her friends and having so much wild success that she sells her company one day for a billion dollars. Then she opens her eyes and begins to think about all the ways she can make that lofty dream a reality. First she meets with professionals in the business. Then she begins to develop a sustainable business model and even sends her ideas off to a friend who specializes in branding. Just this week she sent me a picture of a bottle with her beautiful logo on the front. She is making it happen! She knows it's a big, bold dream, and she knows the learning curve is steep, but that doesn't mean it's out of reach. It may take years of hard work before she holds a bottle of her own brand of bourbon in her hands, but she's willing to work hard to get there. That's inspiring, isn't it? I love being surrounded by dreamers! The risk is thrilling and makes life so exciting. My friend could have kept her dream to herself—too embarrassed to admit it out loud or too worried about what others might think—but instead she decided to chase it, unafraid and unashamed.

I wonder what your big, bold, and beautiful dream might be. What does a happy beautiful life look like for you? When you close your eyes and envision your future reality, who is standing by your side? What are you holding in your hands? Where in the world are your feet planted?

Ask for Help

Maybe you're reading this and don't know where to start. Your present reality is so overwhelming that you don't have the time or space to even begin dreaming about the future. Your goal is to simply survive another day. If that's you, then I just want to say I see you. I've been there, so I know what it's like to feel stuck in a limited season of life. My life is limited in numerous ways. My time is limited by my three young children. I try to squeeze in as much meaningful work as I can while the boys are at school from eight a.m. to two p.m. every day, and sometimes I pick it right back up after they go to bed. My life is also limited by my marital status. As a widow, I don't have a partner to share the load with, so all the responsibility falls on my shoulders. I'm spinning so many plates in the air that at any moment, it feels like they could all come crashing down. So much is riding on me, my own efforts, and my energy tank.

Or maybe you aren't limited by a season of life, but you are limited by your emotional pain. Maybe your pain is so overwhelming that you haven't dared to dream beyond the destruction of your reality. Maybe dreaming even feels like dishonoring your pain. Whatever you are on the other side of, I just want to encourage you. It's okay if you aren't ready to dream again, and it's okay if you need to ask for help so you can have the space you need to dream. To dare to dream beyond the destruction is as much a personal process as it is collaborative. It's okay to hire the babysitter so you can have a night off. It's okay to hire a house cleaner so you take a day off of scrubbing floors and toilets. It's okay to ask Grandma or Grandpa to watch the kids for the weekend so you can take a few days to rest, dream, or just catch your breath. It's okay to say no to the invitation or the extracurricular activity so you can say yes to rest.

This book was a group effort. I didn't write this thing on my own; I asked for help! Grandparents took turns watching the kids for the weekend so I could get away to write. Friends picked up my kids from school so I could spend a few extra hours typing away on my computer. I hired a babysitter to watch my boys for the day so I could work at a local coffee shop. I know my limitations. I know there are some seasons in life when I just can't do it all, and I know it's okay to ask for help. There are so many people who love you, who would be more than willing to step in or step up to support you in your dreams; it just might take laying down your pride and being willing to ask for help. Friend, your dreams are worth the help it might take to achieve them.

The Pursuit of Happiness

An incredible movie called *The Pursuit of Happyness* premiered in 2006. It is based on a true story of a man named Chris Gardner and his journey from being a homeless father on the streets of San Francisco to a wild success on Wall Street. I have seen this movie a handful of times, and after every single viewing, I am a mess of tears and tissues. There are so many powerful moments throughout the story, but there is one in particular that gets me every time. Chris Gardner, played by Will Smith, is playing basketball and having a conversation about life with his young son on a rooftop court overlooking the city of San Francisco. After explaining to his son that he probably won't turn out to be a very successful basketball player, he sees how his words totally shift his son's behavior and steal away his joy. So he pauses, looks his son straight in the eyes, and says, "Hey, don't ever let somebody tell you you can't do something. Not even me, all right? You've got a dream? You've got to protect it. People can't do something themselves, they want to tell you you can't do it. You want something? Go get it, period."[1]

On your journey to rebuilding a beautiful life, some people will try to get in the way of your dreams. Some people won't agree with the decisions you make for your family. Some people want nothing more than for you to stay stuck right where you are because it makes them feel safe. Some people will tell you that your dream is too ambitious or that your timing isn't right. Some people will be offended when your dreams aren't the ones they would have picked out for you. To chase your big, beautiful dream, you have to protect it, be willing to stick with it, and do everything you can to "go get it, period." Life is too dang short to spend it catering to the dreams other people have for you. Your dreams are beautiful because they are yours! Be willing to go to bat for them! Be willing to make the big move or take the big chance anyway! Be willing to say, "This is the way I'm going, with or without your support." Be willing to chase every single dream, big or small, outrageous or ordinary. You only get one life, so live it well!

> Life is too dang short to spend it catering to the dreams other people have for you.

God-Size Dreams

The truth is, we were designed to dream. If we believe we are made in the image of God (Gen. 1:26–27) and that the Creator of the universe breathed life into our lungs, then we all have limitless potential. There is creativity pulsing through our veins; we are all image bearers, mirrors of the divine. To dare to dream beyond the destruction is to be brave enough to look in the mirror and see all these infinite possibilities. The same God that created billions of galaxies in the universe created you and me.

Since that day at the Wailing Wall, I've chased after that "happy beautiful life." I published my first book, I went on my first date, I moved to a new city, I pursued new friendships, I took on new renovation projects at my home, and I even started my own podcast! And I'm not finished yet. I am still here. I am still dreaming about the future. I am still taking action on those dreams. I'm right in the middle of the process—showing up, dreaming big, and working hard to make those dreams come true! Friend, your dreams don't have to be dreams forever. Your dreams can become your reality. You are here right now. You were made for this moment. God has already planted a dream in your heart, so go get it. It matters because it's yours!

CHAPTER 11

OCEAN OF FEAR

There is only one thing that makes a dream
impossible to achieve: the fear of failure.

—Paulo Coelho

It all started through a conversation with my friend Amy's
dad, Don, who said, "I have a guy." To which I responded,
"Huh?"

"When are you going to move down here to the beach?" he
shot back. "I have a guy that can help you out with a loan." A little
dumbfounded and totally uncertain, I said, "Really?"

"Yes, I'll have him call you next week!"

I laughed a little and said, "Sounds great!" Then I didn't

think much of it. I knew in my heart that a life near the ocean had been calling me for a long time, and I figured we would eventually move closer to the sea, but I didn't see it coming so soon. It was August 2020; I had only been working as a writer for about a year and a half. It takes at least two years of holding down a steady job in a profession to qualify for a conventional home loan, and homes at the beach aren't cheap. Moving felt like some far-off, unattainable dream. Maybe he had a guy, but there was no way his guy would qualify a widow and a rookie writer like me.

Turns out I was wrong. His guy called me the following week, and by the weekend I was touring homes in the Spanish village by the sea, also known as San Clemente.

I fell in love with one home in particular. It was a small beach cottage nestled in the Trestles district of town, which meant it was just a short bike ride away from the world-class surf of uppers and lowers at Trestles Beach. An elementary school was only a short walk away too. Plus, it had a garage that was converted into an ADU (additional dwelling unit), which meant my mortgage payment every month would basically be covered by rental income. It was perfect: an affordable way for me as a sole provider and single mother to support an expensive lifestyle at the beach. The house was also absolutely adorable. It had been remodeled from head to toe—a true beach cottage with original wood floors, a chandelier made of seashells, a big open deck with a peekaboo ocean view, a large backyard, a brand-new beautiful kitchen, two large bedrooms (one for me and one large enough to accommodate my three boys), and even a tree in the front yard with a little wooden ladder built into it, perfect for the boys to climb. It had been on the market for months, so the odds of having my offer accepted were high.

They were ready to sell, and I was ready to buy; the only problem was my current home hadn't even hit the market. If I wanted to put in a serious offer on this beautiful beach cottage, I would need to sell my home fast! So I did. I called my realtor, and by the following weekend, we had multiple offers on my house. It was all lining up perfectly. We put in our offer on the beach house, accepted a solid offer on my house, and were ready to rock and roll. It felt like God had ordained the entire plan because everything was falling into place so quickly. It all felt a little too good to be true.

Well, I was right; it *was* a little too good to be true. Someone made a noncontingent offer on the beautiful beach cottage, and the sellers had accepted it. I was devastated. I fell to my knees and cried. In my mind I had already moved into that house. I could see it so clearly: the bunk beds in the back bedroom, the boys climbing the tree in the front yard, walks to school every morning, and bike rides to the beach. All those dreams came crashing down, and I wondered, *God, what does this mean? Are you saying no? Do I keep pushing the door down, or is the door being slammed in my face?*

The next day I took my current home off the market and decided to take a few weeks to pray and wait. Moving would be a big deal. I was already living in a wonderful home that I had just finished remodeling, and it was just down the street from my family and some of our closest friends. The boys were enrolled in an amazing private Christian school. Moving to the beach would mean leaving all those things behind. It would mean living farther away from family. It would mean public school for my boys. And it would mean new friends and new community for all of us. I felt sick to my stomach. I wondered if this dream was worth chasing after all.

Facing the Fear of Big Dreams

The prevailing emotion I experienced as I chased after this deep longing for a new life in a new city was fear. For months I suffered from sleepless nights—sick to my stomach, chest tight with anxiety, and mind racing in a million directions. I wondered, *Am I making a huge mistake? Can I handle this?* The thing about fear is that it's really loud. We become overwhelmed with uncertainty because we can't anticipate the outcome. The fear of failure or the fear of getting hurt or the fear of hurting others is real.

I feared moving to the beach would put me in over my head financially. I was also afraid that this decision would hurt or disappoint the people I loved because we'd be moving away from them. Both of those fears were legitimate. It was a big leap financially, but the ADU setup could make the cost of living sustainable. The idea of moving also caused tension with several family members—so much so that I had to take a step back from some relationships so I could step forward with a decision I knew was in the best interests of my family. I had to let go of the dreams other people had for me in order to live out the dreams I believed God was calling me to.

The truth is, as we begin to take action on our dreams, the process might scare us or even others around us. We may feel overwhelmed with negative emotions or feedback from people who don't agree with our decision or fully support our dreams. With all this noise happening around us, we may even want to throw in the towel. It takes great courage and tenacity to stand our ground against our own inner critics as well as the outer critics, such as the differing opinions of family or friends.

> I had to let go of the dreams other people had for me in order to live out the dreams I believed God was calling me to.

If your close circle of loved ones doesn't understand or support your vision for your dream, here are some steps worth taking with them.

1. Create Space for a Conversation

People are often afraid of things they do not understand, so sitting down and having a vulnerable conversation about the whole picture can often help your loved ones see the intentions of your beautiful dreams. In a safe space, you can ask questions about the fears your loved ones have for your future. You can even acknowledge the pain that this decision may cause them and ask questions about how to support their feelings as you move forward.

2. Offer a Compromise

If that doesn't work, you can always offer a compromise. For example, I told our loved ones, "If the move doesn't work out, I can always move back." I also reassured them that I was still planning to see each of them just as often as we saw them before. I told them how much I valued our relationship and that this move wouldn't change that. Think through what compromises you might be able to offer. How can you involve them in the decision? If the relationship is valuable, how can you still create space and time for connection if you are moving away? How can you invite them into the future with you so they don't feel left behind? These are very tender conversations, but they can be so helpful in finding common ground.

3. Set New Boundaries

If a conversation doesn't provide clarity, or if you can't seem to find common ground, you may need to reevaluate the relationship and create some healthy, new boundaries. Perhaps the boundary is simply conversational. You decide there are certain topics you will no longer discuss during your time together. Or, maybe the boundary is time. As it turns out, you don't owe anyone anything. You don't "have to" do things you don't want to do. If Sunday dinner with your family is a recurring nightmare, you don't have to go to Sunday dinner anymore. If you dread spending time with that group of friends, you can say no to the invitation. If you want to start new traditions for your family during the holidays, you can! If the relationship has become so toxic that you need to take a step back completely, you can do that too! It's okay to say, "I need some space, but I'll be in touch when I'm ready." If someone is consistently unsupportive, you may just need to put a pause on the relationship until they can have a change of heart. Chances are, once your loved ones see you living out your beautiful dreams, they will want to be a part of them.

Sometimes people just can't see the whole picture right away, especially if they are in their own difficult season of loss or grief. This new change could feel like compounding loss—just another thing to grieve. As you know, grief is messy, complicated, and unique; and everyone is on their own timeline when it comes to grief. The best thing you can do is have an abundance of grace in the grieving process and know you can't compare your grief or control how others will grieve. If you feel like others are turning your dreams into nightmares, it's okay to set some new boundaries to protect your beautiful dream!

Finding Your Spark

As we push through the fear of letting others down, we are still left to face our own fears. Our fear of change is often based on the lies, both real and imagined, that we may believe about our dreams: the lie that we aren't capable or qualified; the lie that we will fail if we try; the lie that our loved ones' criticisms are right; the lie that our dreams are too big or too far out of reach. This is where we must let go of the lies. This is where we take back the power of our story. We get to grab the pen and write the next line. We aren't starting a whole new book; we are just writing a new chapter. The last chapter of our life ended with the loss—the divorce, the death of a dream, the career collapse, whatever it may be. Even though it ended, this is where the story gets good. We get to decide what happens next. If we are still alive, we get to dream!

To begin to dream new dreams, we have to grieve the loss of the old dreams first. In my grief journey, I had to grieve not only my husband but also the hundreds of dreams I had attached to him. The dream of growing old together, the dream of doing ministry together, the dream of raising kids together, the dream of traveling together . . . The list feels infinite. I am still in the process of letting those dreams die so I can nurture new dreams. The truth is, new dreams need space and time to grow; they don't grow overnight. We have to let the ground rest before we can start planting new dreams. It may take a while for new ideas, new dreams, or new versions of creativity to come alive in us, but when they do, we will know!

> To begin to dream new dreams, we have to grieve the loss of the old dreams first.

The dream of writing came alive much quicker for me than I anticipated, and it has carried with it a bit of creative mystery. At some moments, the words come at such a fast speed that I feel compelled to stop whatever I am doing to write them down. If I'm driving my car, I will pull over to the side of the road. If I'm going for a run outside, I will run back home or grab my phone and start typing the words out before they are gone. In these moments, I don't want to miss the creativity. I know something special within me is happening that's demanding my attention, and if I don't give it the attention it needs, it will leave. And I don't want it to leave! I want to write it all down and be blown away by it. This doesn't happen every day or all the time, so when it does, it's truly such a treat. I think this is how it is for any creative person. The creativity doesn't always flow freely, so in those magical moments when it does, we just get to stand back in awe of the mystery, grateful for the small role we have to play in it all.

Friend, take as much time as you need to find your spark again. Take time to let the old dreams die so the new dreams can grow healthy and strong. Try new things; chase your big, bold, beautiful dreams. Don't let anyone get in your way—not even yourself. This is your one wonderful shot at life, so don't miss it. Don't miss the beautiful invitation to step into some of your wildest dreams. Show up for yourself right here, where you are! Listen to the creative spirit that is flowing within you and around you. Give your undivided attention to new dreams being birthed within you. You may even be surprised by the beautiful ideas and dreams that come your way!

Back to the Beach House

So there I was curled up in a ball on my bed, shaking from fear and crying because I didn't get the house I wanted. I wondered if I should keep pushing the door down or if this was the universe slamming the door in my face. And I decided: *To hell with the*

131

door. It's time to move. It's time to let the old dream of raising a family with my husband die so I can truly rebuild a new life in a new city without constantly being reminded of a life that's no longer mine.

So I put my house back on the market and started to look for another place by the beach. And guess what? I found another house. It wasn't nearly as perfect as the first house; the price tag was higher, the list of necessary repairs was longer, the kitchen and bathrooms all needed to be renovated and updated, and there were termites everywhere. But I saw beautiful potential hiding beneath the surface. It promised plenty of space for us to host family and friends. The detached garage could easily be converted into an ADU. The location was even closer to the beach, the boys could still go to a great elementary school, and the home was even bigger than the last. Would it be more work? Yup! Would it take more money? Of course! But could I make it a beautiful and functional home over time? Certainly!

I put in an offer, it was accepted, and that big lofty dream became a reality. Was I still terrified? Absolutely! But I moved forward with the dream anyway! Sometimes we have to tell our fears, "I know you're here, but you aren't getting in my way." And it's been the absolute best move I could have ever made for my family. We bought our home just in time, before the market escalated to prices wildly out of reach. My boys and I have made tons of new friends and already feel like we are a special part of this tight-knit community. I am no longer bombarded with grief wherever I go, and it no longer feels like I am living in a cemetery. Everything here is new to us—not tainted by death or grief.

It feels like I can finally breathe again. This is new ground I can build on. This is what new life on the other side of loss should be. We are genuinely happy soaking up the swirling, salty breeze as it blows through our new home and our new life at the sea. What a gift it is to have fought hard to be here. I am so glad I pushed through my fears and the fears others had about my dream.

Friend, your dreams are worth fighting for! If you feel like you are surrounded by loss or living amid the death of a dream, or maybe you, too, are living in a cemetery, you don't have to stay camped out there for another day. Beautiful dreams are waiting for you on the other side of loss. You might just need to be brave enough to search for them until you find them. I truly believe God has beautiful plans for your life—"plans for good and not for disaster, to give you a future and a hope" (Jer. 29:11 NLT). From a friend who thought she'd lost it all, please know that God's promise is true. You haven't lost it all. You are still here! This isn't the end of your story; it's the start of a new chapter, and you, my friend, are holding the pen. What do you want your story to be?

CHAPTER 12

I CHOSE THIS

Everyone has oceans to fly, if they have the
heart to do it. Is it reckless? Maybe. But
what do dreams know of boundaries?
—Amelia Earhart

It was November 2020; the boys were tucked into their beds, and I was cleaning up the usual nightly mess. Picking up the toys scattered across the living room floor and placing them in a pile to be put away the next day. Working my way through stacks of dishes in the sink and wiping down the tabletops and countertops covered in sticky fingerprints, crayons, and remnants of food. Closing curtains and checking each door to make sure it was locked and secure. Unpacking and repacking lunch boxes for the next day. All the rhythms of running a home, the never-ending tasks that build up each day. The long, fast, full days of raising kids.

After all the nightly chores were finished, I stood in the living room staring at the fire roaring in the fireplace and the Christmas tree sparkling in the corner. (Yes, we are the family who decorates for Christmas in November.) And I had a moment of clarity. When my old life died, I was handed a new life I didn't choose. Honestly, it was a life I would never have chosen. My hard, pain-filled reality didn't resemble much of a life at all; for the first few years, it felt like everything was touched by death. Every part of me. Every ounce of my reality. Every single day. All I could think about for a while was how death stole my life. But that night as I was cleaning up the house and shutting it down for the day, I came to the realization that—for the first time in a few years—I was standing in a life I had chosen. I even said the words out loud: "I chose this."

I actually chose this. I chose to move to the sea. I chose a fresh start. I chose to chase a deep-felt dream. I fought hard through overwhelming grief, pain, and fear to get here, but I am in a place I never thought I would be. And I *chose* it; it didn't just happen to me. And this powerful awakening within me as I was cleaning up the house brought me to tears. Death sometimes steals our entire life, but when we hang on, when we push through, when we fight to rebuild again and again and again, we are choosing to take back our lives.

Shaking Off the Victim Mentality

The fight to rebuild doesn't happen overnight. Our fight is made up of the daily choices that, over time, create a life that's beautiful again. It is estimated that the average adult makes about thirty-five thousand choices every day. Broken down, that's about two thousand choices per hour or one choice every couple of seconds.[1] We are bombarded with a never-ending stream of choices from the moment we wake up in the morning until the moment our heads hit the pillows at night. *What should I have for breakfast? What should I wear to work? What time should I leave my house? What route should I take to get to where I need to be?* The internal questioning never stops, and our daily choices, both big and small, add up over time. Eventually they become our habits—both conscious and subconscious, wanted and unwanted. In the words of John C. Maxwell, "Life is a matter of choices, and every choice you make makes you."[2]

When a curveball comes our way, we can often feel like powerless victims of our circumstances. These feelings make it incredibly easy to develop a victim mentality. Most people would never approach the grieving widow or grieving mother and tell her it's time to move on. No one ever came to me and said, "Kayla, Andrew's been gone for a while now. It's time to let it go." I could have stayed camped out in the cemetery for decades, and no one would have even batted an eye. It's an important step in the grieving process to acknowledge the events that caused us to feel powerless, but it's equally important to eventually choose to take back the power. Yes, that hard, awful thing happened, but it doesn't have to define our lives anymore. We have the power to choose how we want to rebuild; we don't have to stay victims of our circumstances. Here are some steps we can take to break free from the victim mentality.

1. Take Ownership

First, we can take ownership of our emotions, desires, and needs. This is the moment we decide to stop blaming others, determine what we want, and chase it. This isn't about pleasing other people; this is about doing what's in our own best interests so we can move forward with our lives.

2. Ask: Why Do I Feel This Way?

Next, we can get curious about our own feelings of powerlessness. When we are blaming other people, God, or the universe for our circumstances and suffering, we aren't actually helping ourselves feel better. Saying things like, "The universe is out to get me," "Nothing good will ever happen for me," or "God must hate me," will only intensify our pain and keep us trapped. When we gently surrender our victim mentality, we are choosing to let go of a story defined by bitterness, anger, distorted perspectives, and unhealed pain. We are choosing to write an entirely different narrative. The question we can stop and ask ourselves in the midst of rebuilding beautiful is: "Do we really want to be healed?"

This question isn't novel. Even Jesus asked this question to those who were suffering. In the gospel of John, we see an interaction between Jesus and a man who had been an invalid for nearly forty years. The man spent decades lying beside the pool of Bethesda—hoping and believing like many other ill, lame, or disabled people that the waters of the pool would offer miraculous healing. It was believed that angels from time to time would stir up the water, and that the first people in the pool after the disturbance would be cured of their ailments. Jesus walked up to this man, knowing his awful condition, then asked him point-blank: "Do you want to be healed?" (John 5:6 ESV). Through this

> The question we can stop and ask ourselves in the midst of rebuilding beautiful is: "Do we really want to be healed?"

question, Jesus established for all of us that the first step toward healing and wholeness is always a deep desire for it. I wonder how many times God has whispered these same words in our ears: "Do you want to be healed?"

The man, exhausted from years of suffering, responded to Jesus with a list of excuses: "I wait, *like all of these people*, for the waters to stir; *but I cannot walk. If I am to be healed in the waters*, someone must carry me into the pool. Without a helping hand, someone else beats me to the water's edge each time it is stirred" (John 5:7 THE VOICE). Basically he did what so many of us are guilty of doing in our own pain. We wallow in the victim mentality because it's easy to look out and find someone else to blame or assume we were just handed bad luck in life. It's a lot harder to take back the power of our circumstance. It's a lot harder to declare that yes, this is the way things are, but it isn't the way things always have to be.

3. Rise in Power

I love Jesus' response to the man: "Get up! Pick up your mat and walk" (John 5:8). He didn't even address the list of excuses; he healed him right on the spot. And the man miraculously did just that. He stood, picked up his mat, and walked! To choose to stand up after life knocks us down is to rise in power. To pick up our mat and walk is to take ownership over our healing. The invalid man could have stayed on the ground, but he didn't. Instead, he chose to stand up and take the first step toward healing.

> The suffering we've experienced can transform into compassion and empathy for others.

When we don't take ownership of our pain, we begin to view our entire lives through victim-tinted glasses. Our pain becomes the only thing we can see. To let go of the victim mentality, we must acknowledge our suffering, show up for the hard work of healing, and then begin to shift our focus. This pain we've been handed can become a beautiful purpose. The suffering we've experienced can transform into compassion and empathy for others. Our healing can give us hearts of forgiveness as we choose to let go of the power that unforgiveness once held over us.

Friend, you are not powerless. You get to choose how long

you play the role of victim. Yes, something horrific really happened to you, and it's an absolute tragedy that it did; but tragedy doesn't have to define your life. You can choose to rise above your circumstance and take the first step forward toward a life that's meaningful and beautiful. You can choose to flip the script and become the victor instead of the victim. I deeply believe that you can get to the place where you wake up in the morning and actually want to pull back the covers and get out of bed. Imagine a day when your daily choices to rebuild your life have added up over time, you look at your surroundings, and you declare—just as I did that night in my living room—"I chose this. This didn't just happen to me." I believe all of us can get to a place on the other side of loss where we truly love our lives again. From there, we can look back and see the butterfly effect of our tragedy. How life has changed and morphed from that pivotal tragic incident or circumstance into something completely different. And how something completely different is deeply beautiful in its own unique way—a vastly different kind of beautiful than before.

Celebrating the Wins

When we pause long enough to look around us and see that we are living in a realized dream—that we are standing in a life we worked hard to rebuild—it's time to stop and celebrate. We did it! We pushed through pain, grief, and fear to get here, but we are here! We are living in a reality that once felt like a far-off dream. You wanted to get remarried, and you did! You wanted to start a family, and you finally are holding a baby in your arms. You wanted to write a book, and you just sent off the manuscript to the publisher. You have been saving up for years to buy a home, and you just received the keys. You went back to school to pursue a college degree, and you made it to graduation day. Arriving at a realized dream is a really big deal. We have to stop, savor, and celebrate the wins.

The victories will carry us through the space in between each realized dream. Text your friends and say, "We're going out!" Schedule the babysitter and book a massage, a night away, or maybe even a spa day. Pop open the bottle of champagne and say cheers to all the hard work it took to get there. Take a day off and have a movie marathon. It isn't selfish to celebrate success.

When we stop long enough to celebrate the wins both big and small, we are activating the reward centers in our brains that release dopamine and energize us with feel-good emotions. This release helps us not only feel good in the moment but also motivates us to carry on and achieve even more. Recognizing victories is about setting off positive chain reactions for even greater dreams down the road.[3]

The wins don't always have to look big, like buying a house, getting married, writing a book, or graduating college. The little wins in life matter too. A win can look like any everyday success, such as: making the bed in the morning, waking up an hour early, getting the kids to bed on time, making a homemade meal, going for a walk around the block, or even mowing the lawn. Each small win fills us with motivation to take on the next task and the next task, until we can step back and take stock of all we've accomplished. Over time, small wins can change the trajectories of our lives.

A small win might look like having the courage to get out of bed in the morning, only to return to bed an hour later. Or maybe a small win will be getting the kids to school on time as a solo or single parent. A small win is as simple as finishing a book you've been wanting to read or gathering the strength to go for a short walk outside. Together, these small steps constitute a big step toward healing. Over time, that hour we make it out of bed will turn into two or three hours. Getting the kids to school on time once will turn into a week of on-time arrivals. That one book we've finished will turn into a stack of books, and that one lap around the block will grow into a mile. Healing doesn't happen overnight; be kind to yourself as you show up in even the smallest ways.

In my first few months as a widow, I had only a few goals for the day: get out of bed, take the boys to and from school, and take a shower. Anything else was extra credit. It took time for that list to grow and for my life to resemble much of a life at all. I spent most of those early days reclining on a zero-gravity chair in the backyard of our home. From that chair, I closed my eyes and listened to the life happening all around me. The sound of the tall eucalyptus trees blowing in the wind. The birds chirping off in the distance. The gardeners busily mowing and landscaping the neighborhood lawns. The kids laughing and playing in the backyard next door. The trickling sound of water flowing from our fountain. As I took in the gentle hum of life, I couldn't fathom ever being able to join in the beautiful sound again. How could I when the song in my heart felt so sad?

It took time for me to realize I had a new song to sing. My daily reality would never look the way it did before, but that didn't mean I had to sit on the sidelines anymore. Life was inviting me to join in the harmony, to squeeze every ounce of good I could out of the awful hard. I didn't have to find all the perfect words right away, or even know how the next day would go; I just had to stand up, pick up my heavy heart, and step toward the beautiful healing I believed was waiting for me. And, friend, I believe that same healing is waiting for you too. Let's chase it together. Let's celebrate all the beautiful wins! Let's dare to dream beyond the destruction. Let's let go of the victim mentality and rise in power. We are still here. Our hearts are still beating strong. We get to choose how we will join in the harmony of life and sing a new victory song!

LIVE

(intransitive verb): to be alive;
to continue alive; to have a
life rich in experience[1]

On the Saturday before Easter 2021, I was out for a run near Zion National Park in Southern Utah. The sun was slowly setting on the majestic bright orange and red mountains as I ran from my great-grandma's house all the way through the gates of the park. As I ran, I was reminded of a picture I had taken of Andrew just a few years before. He was standing in Zion with his arms raised high in the sky, surrounded by the breathtaking views of that day. I decided I had to go back to that same spot and snap another picture, so I did.

As I scrolled through my phone, I was surprised at the stark difference between the two pictures. In the picture of Andrew, taken in the summer of 2018, the trees were green and new life was sprouting up everywhere. And in the picture I took that day, it was spring 2021, and everything was still dead and barren from the winter. Not only that, but in the background of the picture, people were wearing masks. So much had changed since the day I snapped the picture of Andrew. Not only had I survived a few years without him, but I was also surviving the ongoing changes of a global pandemic. It was enough for me to pause right there on my run, on that Saturday before Easter, to embrace the idea that seasons change. That life changes. That even the cycles of nature remind us that nothing lasts forever. Even though our circumstances may feel like the Saturday in between Good Friday and Easter morning—when everything is dark and uncertain—new life is coming. A brand-new version of beautiful is just around the corner. That's what this section of the book is about. It's about embracing changes in our bodies, choosing joy in the midst of the awful hard, and declaring through every changing season that this one life is a beautiful, precious gift!

CHAPTER 13

HABITS FOR SELF-COMPASSION

I believe that the greatest gift you can give
your family and the world is a healthy you.

—JOYCE MEYER

S omeone had stolen the letter *e* from our college cafeteria's sign, so it was known throughout campus simply as "the caf." The caf was a magical place flowing with endless tater tots, cereal, froyo, and soda—the main watering hole for the students of Vanguard University at the time. The place was dangerous: a breeding ground for the infamous "freshman fifteen" (college slang used to describe the extra pounds students tend to gain during their first year of college). All it took was one swipe of my ID card to have access to the all-I-could-eat buffet. It was a jolting shift from life at home with boundaries and parents to the wide-open spaces of a college campus.

Not only did I have access to the caf three times a day, but during my freshman year, it also seemed like most of our fun revolved around food. Late-night stops at In-N-Out Burger for milkshakes and fries, bottomless hot cocoa at the local 24/7 Denny's, and my first job at a popular frozen yogurt joint where I could take home a pint after every shift. I wasn't involved in sports or into exercise at the time, so I was absolutely soaking up all the food and fun. I was destined to be a freshman fifteen statistic, and by the end of the year, my clothes were tighter, my face was a little rounder, and I definitely felt heavier.

I couldn't believe how quickly my body changed. It was honestly a little scary. Without some healthy boundaries in place, I was on a fast track to a very unhealthy lifestyle. So I made a change. I found an active job for the summer as a swim instructor and started to develop better eating and exercise habits on my own.

After that first year of college, I was relieved to never again face struggles with my weight. I knew what steps to take to feel at home in my body and maintain a weight I was comfortable with. I bounced right back after all three of my pregnancies, and I learned to love the rhythms of daily exercise. For years I exercised in our garage gym every single morning, and it became a healthy habit I looked forward to every day. Not only did exercise boost my mental health and physical health, but it also greatly improved my sleep. I was in bed fast asleep by nine p.m. every night. I had three boys under the age of four, and I had never felt more at home in my body.

I was proud of my health and at the top of my game physically. And then, as I encountered deep personal loss for the first time, the daily routines I had worked hard to develop came to a screeching halt.

In the beginning of my journey as a widow, I was so overwhelmed with grief that I lost my appetite completely. I clearly remember sitting on the brown leather couch in the living room of our home as it was filled with a flurry of family and friends. We had just finished saying our final goodbyes to Andrew's body at the graveside, and I was trying my best to be present by engaging in conversations with people who loved my husband. Yet, in my mind, I was disconnected—drifting off as if I was watching myself from a distance. Friends placed plates piled with food near me, hoping I would take a bite, encouraging me to "eat something," but all I could do was stare at the mound of pasta, moving it around with my fork. I wondered if I'd ever enjoy food again, or if I would ever enjoy *life* again. I felt like I was wasting away. I rapidly lost several pounds. I felt frail and weak, not only physically, but mentally and emotionally as well. Andrew's shocking death completely wiped out my health. Everything I had worked hard for over the years—all the muscle I had built in my garage gym, all the strength I had maintained, all the endurance I had gained—drained out of me.

At first the weight loss was welcomed, because in my mind, "coping well" didn't look like gaining weight. I viewed weight gain through a negative lens like so many of us in America. Yet as the time passed and my life significantly slowed down, the scale started tipping in the other direction. I had been a busy stay-at-home mom with an active lifestyle, but now all three of my kids were in school full-time. I started a career as an author, which meant less time moving and more time sitting at a computer typing away. I experienced depression and suicidal ideation, which also physically slowed me down and led to a season of isolation.

Most days I would drop my kids off at school and head straight home to write, read, and rest—all sedentary tasks. My metabolism slowed down with my lifestyle, and I also entered my thirties, a whole new decade. My body no longer responds to small changes in diet and exercise the way it did in my twenties. Then, in the spring of 2020, COVID-19 hit, and we were all forced to slow down and stay home. A stress survey of Americans led by the American Psychological Association found that 42 percent of adults in the United States reported undesired weight gain since the start of the pandemic, with an average gain of almost thirty pounds.[1]

Instead of viewing weight gain as a normal response to an abnormal circumstance, many of us associate it with deep feelings of guilt and shame. We are quick to point the finger at ourselves instead of our circumstance. The weight stigma in America runs deep for men and women, who are bombarded with images of ideal body types everywhere—on the covers of magazines at the grocery store checkout line, in the never-ending scroll through social media, and in the shows we binge on Netflix. It's a constant comparison game. We look at the images, then we look in the mirror, and oftentimes we don't like what we see. At least, that's been the case for me these last few years.

Even if it's unnoticeable to the people around me, I feel ashamed of the weight I've gained during grief and the pandemic. I feel a constant pressure to eat healthy and exercise to keep any additional weight gain at bay. I was recently venting to a close friend about the frustration I've had with my body during this season of life, and she said something very profound. She looked at me and said, "Kayla, you might have been in the best shape of your life when you were married to Andrew, but was that the best version of you?"

Her question has stuck with me ever since. In so many ways, I am proud of the person I am becoming here on the other side of loss. Through my experience with grief, I've given myself permission and freedom to try new things, to pursue new dreams, and to step fully into the person I was created to be! Although my body has changed these last three years, maybe it needed to. Maybe this is the ideal body for this season. Maybe I need to care less about what I look like on the outside and be grateful for the person I'm becoming on the inside. Maybe I need to replace guilt and shame with grace and kindness toward myself. My amazing body has carried me through so much. Why should I think of it only in terms of a number on a scale?

Loss, Trauma, and Physical Health

Though grief is typically discussed in terms of feelings and thoughts, it affects the entire body. Our bodies are hardwired for resilience, but grief still takes its toll and can trigger a multitude of physical health issues. Grief floods our body with stress hormones, and prolonged exposure to these hormone levels can lead to other complications, including physical pain. Some sufferers resort to alcohol or tobacco products to take the edge off the stress and the pain. Overeating or not eating enough is another coping mechanism many of us will endure.[2]

Amid the pain, it's important for us to acknowledge what is happening beneath the surface of our habits. We can self-reflect and ask ourselves: *Why am I reaching for that drink every afternoon? Why am I staring into the fridge looking for something to eat when I'm not even hungry? Why am I having trouble sleeping at night? What is happening in my body? What's the thing beneath the thing?* After the initial wave of grief, shock, and trauma has subsided, let's check in with ourselves. To get to the bottom of our physical health issues and heal our bodies from the inside out, we have to first take stock of the symptoms. If we are having difficulty sleeping, eating, functioning with daily tasks, or maintaining a healthy immune system, it may be time to reach out to a physician or licensed mental health professional. Here are some ways we can fight to get back on track when grief has thrown our bodies out of whack.

1. Step Toward Self-Compassion

Self-compassion is a wonderful first step toward healing. Just as we have compassion for others who are in pain, we should offer the same kindness and understanding to our own suffering souls. To do so is to accept the limits of our own humanity and the limits of our challenging circumstances. One question we can ask ourselves as we practice self-compassion is: *How can I tenderly and gently care for myself in this moment?* We are our own worst critics. We are quick to look in the mirror and ruthlessly judge and scrutinize what we see. But the truth is, we are precious, honored, and loved right here, right now, just as we are. We have to accept the truth of our worth, honoring and loving our bodies for all they have carried us through. And they will continue to carry us through as we fight to find new ways forward!

Self-compassion is not self-pity. Self-pity says, "I am the only one who is suffering," while self-compassion acknowledges, "My suffering is a share of the greater suffering of all humanity." Self-compassion is also not self-indulgence. Just because we are compassionate with our suffering and circumstance doesn't mean we let ourselves fall victim to unhealthy habits. It would be so easy for me to overeat, oversleep, overspend, or overindulge on just about anything, excusing myself by saying, "Well, my husband died, so I deserve this." There is absolutely a time and place in grief to stop and celebrate the wins; but if we give in to self-indulgence on the daily, then we aren't really doing ourselves any favors. We are only creating greater problems for our future selves.

2. Set Realistic Goals

Once we step toward self-compassion, we can start setting small, realistic goals. If we have a habit of eating out four nights a week, we can cut it down to one or two. If we have the habit of overspending on online shopping to numb the pain, we can set budgets. If we implement small changes, over time we are more likely to succeed at the bigger goals we've set for ourselves. We can also establish new routines. Those old routines that used to work were totally disrupted and most likely don't fit into our present life anyway. So what are some new daily rhythms we can work toward? If waking up early to exercise doesn't work anymore, maybe we can head to the gym on our lunch break or schedule a class at our favorite studio in the afternoon.

One area that has been difficult for me in this new life is sleep. I just don't sleep the way I used to. I'm still adjusting to sleeping alone, and I almost always fall asleep watching a show on my phone. It also takes me longer to fall asleep and stay asleep, which leads to exhaustion the next day. A small change I would really like to work toward is establishing a new bedtime routine and falling asleep without the help of my phone. This small change could lead to huge improvements in my energy levels and overall health each day. I just have to be willing to try. And I think that's the key for all of us: to make a small change, we all have to start somewhere, and it begins with our willingness to try.

As we focus on rebuilding our physical health, let go of a specific number on the scale and instead focus on the things that truly matter—such as nutrition, exercise, and sleep. I know the

Self-pity says, "I am the only one who is suffering," while self-compassion acknowledges, "My suffering is a share of the greater suffering of all humanity."

number on my scale will most likely never look the same as it did before, and I have to remember that a number is just a number. It doesn't get to dictate my worth, value, or progress. To work toward the best version of myself here in this new life, I need to let go of my own weight stigma and former beliefs of success. Those rules no longer apply. I will never be satisfied with my body if I'm constantly trying to squeeze it into a framework that doesn't fit anymore.

3. Know Your Worth

To reach a place of self-acceptance where we honor, respect, and treasure the skin we are in, we need to recognize our intrinsic value and worth. To be human is to be uniquely designed to embody the divine. We are "fearfully and wonderfully made" (Ps. 139:14), and that's enough! If I believe that everything God creates is good, then I have to believe he is looking at me just as I am, right here and now, and declaring that I am "very good" (Gen. 1:31). To embrace my body is to embrace all its urges, flaws, and temptations as a gift from God. Even the parts of me that are hard to live with are entwined within the good gift. Fostering a heart of gratitude is the way we counteract our innate human desires to overregulate our bodies. Here is a prayer we can whisper through our feelings of inadequacy:

> God, thank you for the gift of this body with all its flaws, strengths, struggles, and imperfections. I embrace my brokenness and my own temptation to tear apart what you have already declared as good. Give me eyes to see

the beauty hidden within the body you have so graciously given to me as a home for the mystery of your living presence.

Embracing Change

Our bodies are supposed to change. When we were children, these changes were celebrated and praised. In our home, I track how much my boys have grown on their birthday every year. I pull out a Sharpie while the boys stand tall, and I make a little mark under their name on the pantry door in our kitchen. I write their age next to the little mark, and then we step back to marvel and celebrate how much their bodies have changed. "Look how tall you've grown. You are getting so big! I can't believe how little you used to be." Because I see my boys every day, I don't always notice the change. But it's happening; they are changing and growing rapidly. It makes me wonder: *How am I changing and growing every day too?* Maybe it's not in height, but change is happening. Did you know that trillions of cells in our body are changing all the time? Old cells are dying off to create space for new cells every day. Whether we see it or not, we are hardwired for renewal. Change is a constant part of our being, so it's no wonder our bodies look different than they did before. We are being transformed every day.

Maybe you are suffering from a permanent change to your body and wondering if it's still good. Maybe you have suffered from a lifetime of chronic illness or pain and your body feels very broken. Maybe you have never felt at home in the skin you're in. As we rebuild our lives, perhaps it's time to find new ways to welcome and embrace the things we cannot change. Friend, I have no idea what it's like to walk in your shoes. I have no idea what it's like to endure the permanent change you are dealing with. I have no idea what it's like to suffer from chronic illness or pain. But what I do know is that your beautiful, incredible body has carried you through so much. You're still here. Your one heart is still beating strong. As you courageously face and embrace all the changes, may you know just how deeply brave you are.

You are rebuilding beautiful. Even if your body isn't the same kind of "beautiful" it was before, beauty is still possible. It has been said that beauty is in the eye of the beholder. And guess what? You are the beholder. You get to take a good look at yourself and declare beauty, even in the interior parts that no one will ever see. Your body is not a mistake. Your self-worth is so much more than your outward appearance. To love and accept yourself is to love and accept your body right now, just as it is. May you choose grace over and over and over again as you embrace your beautiful body through its ever-changing existence.

CHAPTER 14

DEFIANT JOY

Joy is meant to be ours, a joy that is
defiant in the face of this broken world.
—Stasi Eldredge

In the last decade my little family has moved eleven times. Our longest span of time in a single home was three years, and our shortest stretch was six months. Our six-month home was the sacred place where our world crumbled apart and our journey to rebuild beautiful began. Andrew and I found the home in the spring of 2018. It was a custom-built U-shaped single-story with four spacious bedrooms and five bathrooms sitting on an acre of land. It was over-the-top dreamy: a bathroom in every bedroom, a large gourmet kitchen, and a backyard oasis complete with a waterfall, bridge, river, fireplace, and built-in BBQ. It was the kind of home we imagined would be our "forever home"—a phrase I'm sure was birthed on one of those HGTV reality shows to describe the magical dream house you find in the ideal life where nothing bad ever happens. It's a place where you raise kids, grow old together, and live happily ever after. Once you move in, you never have to move again. I was beyond thrilled to have found our "forever home" at age twenty-nine. We had three boys under the age of five, and the property was the perfect playground to raise our young family.

On the outside, I had everything I could possibly desire—a beautiful family, our dreamy home, and a handsome, successful husband—yet my interior life was crumbling. Andrew and I were personally in one of the most challenging seasons of our marriage. He had recently been diagnosed with depression, and we were all learning to live with the instability it ushered into our lives. It was like getting to know a stranger as my husband became unfamiliar to me. Every single day was an emotional roller coaster as his unpredictable mood majorly impacted the temperature of our home. It was also summertime, which meant school was out and our boys were home full-time. Most days I managed the kids on my own as Andrew wrestled with his mental health and rested in our bedroom. We were doing everything we knew to do for him to get better, and I was torn in two trying to be a loving, supportive wife as well as a loving, present mom.

On those long exhausting summer days, the boys and I loved to play in the sprawling dirt lot at the back of our property. I would grab a good book and a cup of coffee, then place my folding lawn chair in the dirt while they let their imaginations run wild. They would dig holes and use the hose to create monstrous mud puddles. They would dress up in their police uniforms and drive their plug-and-play police car around to catch "bad guys." One day they even found old paint buckets, picked up a few sticks, and made their own musical band. Out of all the beautiful spaces our home had to offer, my boys were thrilled just to play in the dirt. While I sat on my lawn chair watching my boys play day after day, I was astonished at their incredible ability to dig up joy in the most unlikely place. They searched for it and found it over and over again. Every day was a thrilling outdoor adventure.

In my own way that summer, I was digging for joy too. I was desperate for it. My reservoir of joy was near empty, and I felt stretched thin by our present reality. I was looking for joy in the external, unaware that I was grasping for air. Turns out joy isn't something you find somewhere out there; it's something you uncover inside. You have been invited to internal joy every single day—not based on circumstances, not dependent on your emotional state or the emotional state of your spouse, not determined by how many arguments your kids had that day or even how much money you have in the bank. Joy isn't something that happens to us or something we randomly stumble upon; joy is something we choose. One of my favorite authors,

> Joy isn't something that happens to us or something we randomly stumble upon; joy is something we choose.

Henri Nouwen, wrote, "We have to choose joy and keep choosing it every day."[1] To choose this kind of deep-rooted joy is to reside in a reality beyond our present mood or circumstance. Real joy isn't anchored in how we feel in the moment; real joy is anchored in the eternal. To reach for joy is to reach for truth; to reach for truth is to reach for God; and to reach for God is to find him in the ordinary and the extraordinary details of our daily lives.

The Comparison Trap

It has often been said that comparison is the thief of joy. That summer while my kids played in the dirt, I spent much of my time sitting in my lawn chair mindlessly scrolling through my social media news feed. As I scrolled, I grew bitter and angry toward the life right in front of me. The thoughts running through my mind were full of jealousy. *Why can't my husband be more like this husband? Why can't my home look more like this home? Why can't my body look more like this body? Why does my life look so messy and chaotic while this person's life looks perfect? Why do they get to go on a vacation to Hawaii while I'm stuck here playing in the dirt?* While I deeply believe social media can be a beautiful resource, it can also be a battleground for our peace and joy.

We live in an age of extreme envy. There is an envy for everything: relationship envy, home envy, success envy, body envy, and even children envy. If we do not carefully guard our time and protect our hearts, the highlight reels we hold in our hands can become powerful weapons used against us. To chase envy is like trying to catch the wind; our efforts hardly ever yield results, and we are left empty-handed every time. Envy isn't only ugly; it's also dangerous. Psychotherapist Patricia Polledri, author of *Envy in Everyday Life*, powerfully describes the epidemic of envy: "Envy is wanting to destroy what someone else has. Not just wanting it for yourself, but wanting other people not to have it. It's a deep-rooted issue, where you are very, very resentful of another person's wellbeing—whether that be their looks, their position or the car they have. It is silent, destructive, underhand—it is pure malice, pure hatred."[2] That definition of envy is a brutal wakeup call. Perhaps that's why even in the proverbs—written thousands of years before the age of social media—we read that "a heart at peace gives life to the body, but envy rots the bones" (Prov. 14:30).

To rebuild our lives, we must refocus our eyes on what is right in front of us. If envy is eating away at our joy, perhaps it's time to make changes. To combat envy, we must gently name it as an emotion and do our best to understand what that emotion is trying to tell us.

- How can I turn this envy into a positive force that will drive me forward toward goals I'd like to achieve?
- Is my envy rooted in simply wanting what I can't have but can live without?
- Why do I feel an urge to post about my success, my new home, or my new fancy car?
- What is the driving motivation behind my envy?
- Am I contributing to the vicious cycle of envy?

If we were to be brutally honest, most of us would admit that it feels pretty good to receive validation through sharing our successes on social media. When someone likes, comments, shares, or retweets our posts, the reward center of our brain is flooded with feel good emotions. Those feelings of pleasure and satisfaction not only boost our self-esteem but also keep us coming back for more. But are we aware of our own motivations? How much are we emotionally invested in what we post, and what are the returns on our investments? If social media is stealing our peace or "rotting our bones," perhaps it's time to reevaluate how much time and attention we give it.

Joy No Matter the Circumstance

After the loss of Andrew, we moved out of that dreamy home with the big dirt lot and moved in with family. A few weeks later it was my son Smith's sixth birthday, so we decided to throw a big party in the backyard with all his favorite buddies. I was already lost in a sea of conflicting emotions, unsure how I could celebrate my son without my husband by my side. It was the first birthday celebration since his passing, and I was fighting for joy in the midst of my utter despair. Raising kids while grieving is a lesson in defiant joy. With kids, there is no pause button, no sleeping in, and no checking out of responsibilities. My boys have been the driving force of my joy. They have kept me laughing, smiling, and cherishing life amid the heavy hard. Defiant joy doesn't discount our suffering. *Defiant* by definition is rising against the tide, going against the flow, and standing in opposition. To choose joy in the midst of sorrow or suffering is choosing to say "even though." Even though Andrew died, we are still showing up for this one life. Even though I wanted to curl up in my bed and give up completely, I chose to rise. And on my son's sixth birthday, even though we were full of sorrow, we decided to celebrate anyway. We would have the party, sing the birthday song, and celebrate life in the face of death.

In the middle of his birthday celebration, I had another encounter with an "even though." It was late November, and since his party was taking place outside at night, I decided we should light the firepit. I had never lit the firepit before, but I was confident I could figure it out. How hard could it be? I turned on the gas, grabbed the lighter, leaned over the firepit— and the last thing I remember was a loud *whoosh*! The gas was turned on too high, and the flame erupted in my face, catching my hair on

> To choose joy in the midst of sorrow or suffering is choosing to say "even though."

fire. I lifted my arms and quickly put out the flames using the jean jacket I was wearing. Then I walked inside, headed into my bedroom, and cried. I was already standing on the edge of an emotional cliff before my hair went up in flames, and this nearly sent me freefalling into a pit of despair. My mind went straight to my grief: *If Andrew had been here, this wouldn't have happened.*

I couldn't believe my misfortune; I was absolutely mortified. No one would have blamed me if I'd called it a night right then and there, never to emerge from my bedroom again. But I wouldn't let that happen. I would rise in defiance to the moment. I would shout: "Even though my hair caught on fire, I will still show up to celebrate my boy." So I threw on a beanie to cover my charred hair, wiped away my tears, and rejoined our family and friends outside.

This kind of defiance is not denial. Embracing defiant joy doesn't mean ignoring our reality, pretending we are okay when we are not, or attempting to hide our pain. I wasn't denying my embarrassment at having completely fried my hair. I wasn't denying that it was painfully hard to show up and celebrate my son's birthday with my heavy, broken heart. I wasn't trying to pretend I was okay or put on a brave face for anyone. Instead, I was reaching for joy in the midst of my pain, not absent or disconnected from the reality of our circumstance. I wanted to be fully present to the suffering *and* fully present to the joy.

Defiant joy isn't moved by circumstance. When we tap into defiant joy, we aren't tapping into our own reserves; we are reaching for a far greater, richer, more life-giving reservoir altogether. Joy is rooted in God's love for us. In the midst of our greatest suffering, "the joy of the LORD is [our] strength" (Neh. 8:10). When we reach for joy by our own sheer willpower or resilience, we will return empty-handed every time. We don't simply bounce back to beautiful again. To rebuild our lives, we must reach for the unshakeable, immovable, wonderful joy that can only be described as supernatural. It's a mysterious joy that is beyond our understanding, but it's this "beyondness" that makes it so powerful. The world didn't offer it to us, so the world can't take it away.

Unhealthy religion may encourage you to hide, cover up, or escape suffering, but what if suffering isn't something to be avoided? What if suffering is the way through to joy? According to Franciscan tradition, genuine joy "takes place through our pain—not under it, to the right, left, or over it."[3] And to quote one of my favorites, Henri Nouwen, again, "Joy is hidden in sorrow and sorrow in joy. If we try to avoid sorrow at all costs, we may never taste joy."[4] Every moment is an opportunity for joy. That night at my son's sixth birthday party, I searched for the joy and I found it. I found it in the smile on my son's face as he blew out the candles on his birthday cake. I found it in meaningful conversations with friends. I found it in cuddles with my two-year-old son, Brave, as he sat wrapped in a blanket on my lap. I found it in the breathtaking view of the city lights flickering in the dark over the horizon. I smelled like a bonfire, I was terribly sad my husband wasn't there, and I greatly wished our circumstances were different, but none of those things touched my immovable, unshakeable, supernatural, wonderful joy.

Friend, you may wish your circumstance was different. You may never understand why God allowed your pain to be filtered through his mighty hands. But you can still choose joy. You can choose to grab hold of the supernatural amid the natural. You can choose to search for the glimmers of goodness and hope right there in the pit of your pain. To rebuild a life that's beautiful again, joy is the weapon you wield. Right here, right now, your joy can be "a river overflowing its banks" (John 16:24 MSG). Let's chase it together—one breath, one moment, one hour, one day at a time.

CHAPTER 15

IT'S ALL A GIFT

This is a wonderful day. I have never seen
this one before.

—MAYA ANGELOU

I love Christmas. My favorite tradition is to decorate my home on
November 1 and enjoy two full months of holiday magic. I love
the music, the lights, the eggnog, the cheesy pictures with Santa
Claus, and the classic Christmas movies. I love it all. And my
favorite part of the whole holiday season is the thrill of Christmas
morning with my kids. The giggles as they race down the hallway
in their festive PJs to see their presents on display for the very
first time is a sound I look forward to every year. However, there

is one thing I don't like about Christmas: the moment after the mad dash down the hall and the ripping of wrapping paper. All parents brace themselves for this: the moment when the magic is overtaken by unmet expectations. All the presents are opened, wrapping paper remnants are scattered all over the floor, and your kids are complaining that they didn't get what they had wished for.

I was that kid. I was in the eighth grade, and all I wanted for Christmas was a skateboard. I wrote it on my list and showed my parents pictures of the board I wanted. I even pointed at the skateboards on display in the store when we were shopping. The message was loud and clear. That year we were traveling out of town for Christmas, so we opened presents a few days early. I was full of anticipation; I was already mastering tricks in my mind and couldn't wait to skate all over the neighborhood. Yet with each present I unwrapped, my skateboarding dreams began to unravel. Before I knew it, I had opened all my presents and felt utterly ungrateful and disappointed. I didn't get what I asked for, and I tried to hold it in.

The following day, we had a few last-minute errands to run before we left on vacation. One of the places where we stopped was a local sporting goods store called Chicks. And on display, right when we walked in, was a rack of skateboards. I tried my best to hold back my ungratefulness, but by the end of our time in the store, I couldn't take it anymore. As soon as the words came tumbling out of my mouth, I had instant regret.

"Hey, Mom, you know one present that I really wanted but didn't get this year? A skateboard."

She turned and looked at me with fire in her eyes. There she stood, an exhausted mother who had tried her best to make Christmas special. She had purchased the thoughtful presents, booked the trip out of town, and was even trying to cover all her bases by buying my sister and me proper snow clothes. And there I stood, asking for more—unable to see through my immature eyes all that she had already given to me. Her frustrated reaction was well-deserved, and I haven't forgotten the interaction ever since.

I wish I could say I've been grateful ever since that day at the sporting goods store, but that would be far from the truth. The truth is, every day is a fight to see the good, a fight to find the gifts hidden right here in my daily life. Life these days is a flurry of sports, kids, work, and chores. Always somewhere to go, something to do. The mornings are fast—the boys rushing off to learn at school while I quickly switch gears and squeeze in as much meaningful work as possible before the clock tells me it's time to bring them home. And how the time flies? I'm not sure. I blink and the boys are taller, and their pants are suddenly smaller. Their silly smiles are a clutter of missing teeth and giant teeth that one day won't look so giant anymore. My house is over-flowing with noise. Laughter, yelling, squealing, fighting, and wrestling on the living room floor. I feel dizzy as it swirls around me. Life is happening at such a fast speed. I want to soak it up, to be present, to drink it all in, and I'm tired and want to curl up and check out of it all too. These are the long, fast days of raising kids. Maybe I'll remember it all one day, or maybe the point isn't to remember it all—but just to behold it right now as it is.

Beholding the Gift

To *behold* is to see with attention, to observe with care, to fix our eyes. Gratitude is in the details; if we don't slow down long enough to see it, it will surely pass us by. Perhaps the greatest threat to fixing our eyes is our speed. I don't know about you, but I am always in a hurry. I feel like I am constantly shouting at my kids, "Let's go, let's go, let's go! Why are you moving so slow? We are going to be late . . . again!" From the moment my feet touch the floor in the morning, I don't stop running. I feel exhausted all the time. I tell myself it's a season of life, that it won't always be this way. I feel like I'm parenting on autopilot. I'm here, but I'm not here; my mind wanders off, preoccupied on the never-ending list of what's next. Yes, I'm in the backyard answering the call of "Mommy, can you come watch me?" But in my mind I'm also running through the agenda for tomorrow and thinking about dinner, laundry, dishes, and bedtime. You would think sitting on the sidelines would slow me down, but it doesn't. Some days I feel like I'm missing out on my own life. *Where is the off-ramp? Where is the pause button? Will I ever find rest?* I feel ashamed of my own ungratefulness. I have more than enough. Even without a husband, my life is overflowing with good things. *Am I missing something?*

Perhaps to truly behold the gift of life, we need to pump the brakes and slow down our bodies *and* our minds. In his profoundly resourceful book, *The Ruthless Elimination of Hurry,* John Mark Comer says this about the dangers of a hurried life: "Not only does hurry keep us from the love, joy, and peace of the kingdom of God—the very core of what all human beings crave—but it also keeps us from *God himself* simply by stealing our attention. And with hurry, we always lose more than we gain."[1] To cultivate a life of gratitude, we must find new ways to slow ourselves down.

1. Turn Down the Noise

One way we can seek rest in our day-to-day is to turn down the volume. Even though this season of life may be busier than ever, that doesn't mean there isn't room for rest. Even Jesus rested. Throughout the gospels we see Jesus withdrawing to a quiet place to pray. Even when his ministry was booming, he created space to slow down. Through his rhythms of rest and retreat, Jesus modeled for us that rest isn't about waiting out a busy season, but rather about seeking rest amid the chaos, when we need rest the most. I don't need to wait until my boys are older and out of the house to finally get rest. I don't need to wait until the end of the day when the house is quiet again to catch my breath. I don't need to wait until I accomplish the next task at work to finally feel a sense of peace. I can search for ways to slow down right now. Perhaps it isn't so complicated after all. Maybe it's simply choosing not to pick up my smartphone during every empty second of the day. Or maybe it's paying attention to how often I fill the silent spaces with noise, like the radio in the car and the TV at home. I can even take note of the unnecessary noise in my head. When my cluttered mind wanders off to worry about dinner, work, laundry, homework, bills, and all the other unknowns, I can gently work my thoughts back toward the present moment. Perhaps the best way to unlock a life of gratitude is to turn toward the gifts that are right in front of us.

2. Find Time to Retreat

There is a breathtaking place up the coast of California where I love to retreat alone. I've only visited once, but in my mind, I've returned many times. It's a historic, bright yellow bed-and-breakfast that stands tall on the edge of a cliff overlooking the ocean in Pacific Grove, California. There is a walking trail that follows the curve of the cliff for miles, and a quaint town full of mom-and-pop restaurants. It's charming in every sense of the word, and it just happens to be down the road from my favorite spa in the world. On my visit, I savored every moment—the delicious breakfast buffet in the small dining room overlooking the sea, the unhurried walks on the trail, and the glorious spa that I left feeling refreshed from head to toe. In one of the busiest seasons of my life, it is a treat to get away. When I seek the quiet calm and give my soul the gift of slowness, I am filled with gratitude every time. Trips like this are few and far between for me, so I seek the micro version daily: walks on the trail by the sea, slow sips of coffee with friends, surfing on Monday mornings with a group of fellow moms, puzzles by the fireplace with my boys, and extra snuggles at night as I tuck them into bed. Turns out, there are

> Turns out, there are pause buttons hidden everywhere. We're often just too busy to notice them.

pause buttons hidden everywhere. We're often just too busy to notice them.

3. Practice Gratitude Daily

Gratitude isn't a destination; it's a daily practice. One of my favorite ways to practice giving thanks is through writing in my prayer journal. Before I ask to receive anything at all, I make a list of the things I already have. And most of the time, by the end of writing down the gifts I've already received, I don't feel such a deep need to ask for more. God has given me everything I need to live a grateful life right here. I have a roof over my head, a car sitting in my driveway, clean running water, a pantry full of food, and three busy boys running wild and spilling joy into every inch of my home. However, the greatest gift I have—the one I cherish the most—is love. The love I feel when I sit and soak in God's presence. The love I receive from my kids, my family, and my friends. I wonder if love is really all we need. To receive love is to have love to give the world. Our gratitude is an expression of our love.

Gratitude is not only an expression of our love; it is also an indication of our health. Research on the psychology of gratitude found several proven health benefits to the daily practice and cultivation of gratitude. For example, gratitude greatly improves sleep and strengthens our overall well-being, meaning greater overall health and less physical or emotional pain. Grateful people also tend to have higher energy levels, and research has even correlated gratitude with optimism.[2]

The Greek word for gratitude is *chariti*, which means

> To live with a heart of gratitude is to have eyes to see that everything is a gift.

extending favor toward or giving grace. To live with a heart of gratitude is to have eyes to see that everything is a gift. Every single moment, every single day, God is extending undeserved grace. Just as with the gift of love, those who receive abundant grace now have abundant grace to give away.

The Greatest Gift

As I type these words, Christmas is coming again soon. It's almost time to set up the tree in the corner with that crooked star on top, to break out all our festive décor, to bake gingerbread cookies, and to dance to holiday jingles in front of the flames of the fireplace. It's almost time to drive down the street and take in the sights of the homes decorated in twinkling lights. In the coffee shops, restaurants, grocery stores, shopping malls, and even at the end of the San Clemente pier, the message is clear: Christmas is here. An entire holiday season to reflect on the greatest gift of all—when love came near and changed our lives forever.

One of my favorite, dearest Christmas memories is of my husband, Andrew, reading the Christmas story to the congregation at our church. Our sons Jethro and Smith took turns joining their dad on stage to sit on his lap as he read the words from their own little *Jesus Storybook Bible*. The boys giggled and blushed in front of the crowd in the comfort of their father's arms. It was precious.

As we've rebuilt our Christmas traditions on the other side of loss, everything looks so much different than before. We are no longer preparing and working hard toward hosting multiple services at our church. Those days are long gone. "Church" for us now at Christmastime looks less like stepping foot into a building and more like inviting friends into the warmth of our home. For the last two Christmas seasons, a kind and generous friend has gone out of his way to string Christmas lights on our home—the first year in the pouring rain, and last year, literally an hour out of his way on his day off. What a gift. This is a picture of what church looks like for us now. It looks like being in community with friends who, even though it's been a few years, remember that I'm still a widow—not because they feel bad for me, but because they love me and want to serve my little family. Those strings of lights that dance and sparkle on the outside of our home at Christmastime have God's fingerprints all over them. This is what Jesus was getting at when he told us to love our neighbors as ourselves. This is what the church looks like outside the building. And my cup overflows with gratitude.

Although things have changed on the other side of loss, our days are still strikingly beautiful. We are learning to live within and to surrender to the mystery. We are learning to rise every day and unwrap the gifts waiting for us in each present moment. And as we welcome *what is*, dare to dream again, and step bravely into the beauty of *what could be*, we are believing that the possibilities are laced with wonder, hope, and grace. It is a wonderful gift that we are here, right now, in this very moment. We have breath in our lungs, we have life in our bones, and we have everything we need. Friend, you are deserving of a big, beautiful, adventurous life. Keep your head up. Find ways to embrace your pain and show up to do the hard work of healing. Dare to try new things, explore new opportunities, and dream new dreams. Choose gratitude and joy right where you are, and believe that even though your circumstances have changed, you are fully capable of rebuilding a beautiful life. I am so proud of you.

EPILOGUE

A WILD RIDE

I hope you live a life you're proud of. And
if you find that you're not, I hope you have
the strength to start all over again.
—Eric Roth

When I think about the journey of rebuilding beautiful, I can't help but think about my son Jethro's first time on a roller coaster. We were in Northern Idaho visiting friends, and we spent the day together at a local amusement park famous for their colossal wooden rides. All day, Jet was looking forward to his first ever roller coaster experience! If you know Jet, you know he is a planner. He has high expectations for how things should go, and when reality collides with his expectations, the results are intense and expressive. Since he is my most expressive kid, I knew I had to capture his first roller coaster on video. So I did! We slid into our seats, pulled the safety belt tightly in place, and began our climb to the top of the first big drop. I pulled out my phone and filmed Jet's expressions from beginning to end. When we exited the roller coaster and took a good look at the video, I laughed until I cried. It was gold. Captured on my phone was every expression Jethro's little six-year-old body could possibly make. He was happy, excited, and absolutely terrified the whole way through. He was laughing one minute and screaming the next, and at the end of the ride he smiled, let out a big exhale, and threw his hands in the air. What a wild ride!

I wonder how many of us on our journey of rebuilding beautiful feel a bit like my Jethro. We aren't sure how to respond to all the twists and turns and highs and lows on this wild ride of life. But we're still here. We're fully present, strapped in, ready to go, and willing to see it through—all the way to the end. Friend, I am so proud of you for courageously showing up and saying yes to rebuilding a beautiful life! I am so proud of you for stepping toward your pain, showing up for the hard work of healing, and daring to dream again. I am so proud of you for trying the new things, for going on that date, for having those hard conversations, and for choosing joy and hope each day! We've fought hard to get here, and we aren't finished yet.

The thing I'm learning here about life is that we will always be rebuilding. Just when we think we have it all figured out, life will lead us in a new direction. To fight to find a way forward when life breaks our hearts is to keep stepping with shaky feet into the unpredictable unknown. All we have is today. To fully appreciate the gift of today isn't to ignore the past or to look too far into the future; it's simply to behold it all right now, just as it is. We are here. We are rebuilding beautiful. There is so much more ahead! Let's chase it together—one brave day at a time!

ACKNOWLEDGMENTS

Writing *Rebuilding Beautiful* in the midst of a very full but limited season of life took an entire army of support. To my family, thank you for your loving encouragement and support. Thank you for believing in me when I was too tired to believe in myself, and thank you for taking such great care of my three boys so that I could have the space I needed to pen down these words. To my dear friends, thank you for loving me, holding me, crying with me, watching my kids, and cheering me on the whole way through. To my agent, Whitney, my wonderful editor, Jenny, and the entire team at Thomas Nelson, thank you for supporting my vision for this book and for partnering with me once again to release my heart into the world. And to my three beautiful boys, may these words bless your heart one day when you are old enough to read them. Being your mom is the greatest honor and adventure of my life. Thank you for loving me and holding me through this sacred season as I've loved and held you too. What a joy it is to rebuild this life together. I am so proud of us. We're growing up right here every day. What a gift!

FOR REFLECTION

EMBRACE

Chapter 1: Embracing the Unexpected

1. In what ways have you tried to run away from your pain?
2. What unhealthy habits are getting in the way of your ability to lean into your pain?
3. How has shame played a role in your pain?

Chapter 2: Cultivating Community

1. In what ways can you pursue connection and solidarity with others?
2. Who have you allowed to carry your pain with you?
3. What steps can you take to share the weight of your pain?

Chapter 3: Befriending Death

1. If you have lost a loved one, how has death changed your perspective on life?
2. What does acceptance look like for you?
3. Have you found acceptance in this stage of grief?
4. How has your pain moved forward with you?
5. What does it mean to hold space for both sorrow and joy?

HEAL

Chapter 4: Who Am I?

1. As you rebuild your life, what parts of who you were in the past no longer serve you in your present?
2. How have you reclaimed your identity in this season of rebuilding?
3. Who do you want to become?
4. What new passions do you want to pursue?

Chapter 5: A New Narrative

1. In what ways have you planned for the harder calendar days?
2. What does redemption mean to you?
3. How have you seen redemption in the rebuilding process?
4. What new traditions have you established or would like to establish as you move forward?

Chapter 6: Doing the Work

1. How have you engaged with your trauma?
2. What path of healing has been helpful to you?
3. How have your scars become a sacred part of who you are?

EXPLORE

Chapter 7: Worthy of Love

1. How has your loss or pain changed your relationships?
2. Has your suffering changed the way you welcome and embrace love? How?
3. Do you feel worthy of love?

Chapter 8: The Crisis of Faith

1. How has your experience impacted your faith?
2. Have you wrestled with God in your pain? How?
3. What approaches to faith have been healing for you?
4. What does a relationship with God look like here?

Chapter 9: I'm So Proud of You for Trying

1. What new ambitions have piqued your curiosity in this season of rebuilding?

2. What fears are preventing you from trying something new?

3. What small steps forward can you take?

DREAM

Chapter 10: Happy Beautiful Life

1. What does a "happy beautiful life" look like for you?

2. What are your beautiful dreams?

3. How can you ask for help or support in pursuing your dreams?

Chapter 11: Ocean of Fear

1. What fears are getting in the way of your dreams?

2. How have your loved ones responded to your dreams?

3. What fears have they expressed?

4. What boundaries do you need to set in place to protect your beautiful dreams?

5. What lies might you be believing about your ability to achieve your dreams?

Chapter 12: I Chose This

1. Which "I chose this" moments have you encountered on your rebuilding journey?

2. Are you stuck in a victim mentality? If so, what steps can you take to break free?

3. How can you rise in power in the midst of your circumstance?

4. How have you stopped to celebrate your realized dreams?

EXPLORE

Chapter 13: Habits for Self-Compassion

1. How has a season of grief or unexpected loss challenged your physical health?

2. How can you step toward self-compassion and self-acceptance?

3. In what ways can you reach for gratitude and embrace all your insecurities as a beautiful part of the gift of your body?

Chapter 14: Defiant Joy

1. How might comparison be stealing your joy?

2. Describe your relationship with social media. Is it creating an unhealthy cycle of envy?

3. In what ways can you choose supernatural joy amid your challenging circumstance?

Chapter 15: It's All a Gift

1. How can you practice silence and solitude in the midst of your everyday life?
2. If you could get away for a few days, where would you go? What steps can you take to make that getaway dream a reality?
3. In what ways are you practicing gratitude?

NOTES

PART I: EMBRACE

1. *Merriam-Webster*, s.v. "embrace (verb)," accessed March 22, 2022, https://www.merriam-webster.com/dictionary/embrace.

CHAPTER 1: EMBRACING THE UNEXPECTED

1. Carl von Clausewitz, "Friction in War," in *On War*, eds. and trans. Michael Howard and Peter Paret (Princeton, NJ: Princeton University Press, 1989), 55–57.

CHAPTER 3: BEFRIENDING DEATH

1. William Whitaker's Words, s.v. "compatior, compati, compassus (verb)," University of Notre Dame Archives, accessed March 24, 2022, https://archives.nd.edu/cgi-bin/wordz.pl?keyword =compati.

HEAL

1. *Merriam-Webster*, s.v. "heal (verb)," accessed March 22, 2022, https://www.merriam-webster.com/dictionary/heal.

CHAPTER 6: DOING THE WORK

1. Richard Rohr, "Transforming Pain," Center for Action and Contemplation, October 17, 2018, 2022 , https://cac.org /transforming-pain-2018-10-17. Adapted from Richard Rohr, *A Spring Within Us: A Book of Daily Meditations* (Albuquerque, NM: CAC Publishing, 2016), 199, 120-21.

2. Debra Fulghum Bruce, "Exercise and Depression," WebMD, April 1, 2022, https://www.webmd.com/depression/guide /exercise-depression.

3. "What Is Spiritual Direction?," Center for Action and Contemplation, accessed March 25, 2022, https://cac.org/about /what-is-spiritual-direction/.

4. Deborah Siegel-Acevedo, "Writing Can Help Us Heal from Trauma," *Harvard Business Review*, July 1, 2021, https://hbr .org/2021/07/writing-can-help-us-heal-from-trauma.

EXPLORE

1. *Merriam-Webster*, s.v. "explore (verb)," accessed March 25, 2022, https://www.merriam-webster.com/dictionary/explore.

CHAPTER 8: THE CRISIS OF FAITH

1. George Matheson, "O Love That Wilt Not Let Me Go," Hymnary .org, accessed March 26, 2022, https://hymnary.org/text/o_love _that_wilt_not_let_me_go.

2. "What Is Contemplation?," Center for Action and Contemplation, accessed March 26, 2022, https://cac.org/about/ what-is -contemplation/.

DREAM

1. *Merriam-Webster*, s.v. "dream (verb)," accessed March 26, 2022, https://www.merriam-webster.com/dictionary/dream.

CHAPTER 10: HAPPY BEAUTIFUL LIFE

1. *The Pursuit of Happyness*, directed by Gabriele Muccino (2006; London: Sony Pictures Home Entertainment, 2007), DVD.

CHAPTER 12: I CHOSE THIS

1. Eva M. Krockow, "How Many Decisions Do We Make Each Day?," *Psychology Today*, September 27, 2018, https://www .psychologytoday.com/us/blog/stretching-theory/201809 /how-many-decisions-do-we-make-each-day.
2. John C. Maxwell, *Beyond Talent: Become Someone Who Gets Extraordinary Results* (Nashville: Thomas Nelson, 2011), 10.
3. Jessica DuBois-Maahs, "Why You Should Celebrate Small Wins," Talkspace (blog), August 1, 2018, https://www.talkspace.com /blog/why-you-should-celebrate-small-wins/.

LIVE

1. *Merriam-Webster*, s.v. "live (verb)," accessed March 27, 2022, https://www.merriam-webster.com/dictionary/live.

CHAPTER 13: HABITS FOR SELF-COMPASSION

1. Kirsten Weir, "The Extra Weight of COVID-19," *Monitor on Psychology* 52, no. 5 (July 2021): 26, https://www.apa.org/monitor /2021/07/extra-weight-covid.
2. "When Loss Hurts: 6 Physical Effects of Grief," GoodTherapy, May 20, 2018, https://www.goodtherapy.org/blog/when-loss -hurts-6-physical-effects-of-grief-0520187.

CHAPTER 14: DEFIANT JOY

1. Henri J. M. Nouwen, *You Are the Beloved: Daily Meditations for Spritual Living* (New York: Convergent, 2017), 169.

2. Patricia Polledri, quoted in Moya Sarner, "Age of Envy—Social Media Has Created a World in Which Everyone Else Seems Happy," *Irish Times*, October 10, 2018, https://www.irishtimes.com/life-and-style/health-family/age-of-envy-social-media-has-created-a-world-in-which-everyone-else-seems-happy-1.3657251.

3. "Crisis Contemplation and Joy," Center for Action and Contemplation, July 29, 2021, https://cac.org/crisis-contemplation-and-joy-2021-07-29/.

4. Henri J. M. Nouwen, *Bread for the Journey: A Daybook of Wisdom and Faith* (New York: HarperOne, 1997), January 2.

CHAPTER 15: IT'S ALL A GIFT

1. John Mark Comer, *The Ruthless Elimination of Hurry: How to Stay Emotionally Healthy and Spiritually Alive in the Chaos of the Modern World* (New York: WaterBrook, 2019), 25.

2. Courtney E. Ackerman, "What Is Gratitude and Why Is It So Important?," PositivePsychology.com, February 5, 2022, https://positivepsychology.com/gratitude-appreciation/.

ABOUT THE AUTHOR

Kayla Stoecklein became an unexpected widow in August 2018 when her husband, Andrew, the pastor of their large church in California, died by suicide. With three young boys also grieving and a heart full of pain, she began sharing her struggles that she captured in *Fear Gone Wild* (September 2020). It became her mission to bring hope and faith-filled help to others who have faced unexpected hardships, showing them that they not only have a purpose, but that they can build a beautiful life once again.